IMAGES
of America

THE SUTTER
BUTTES

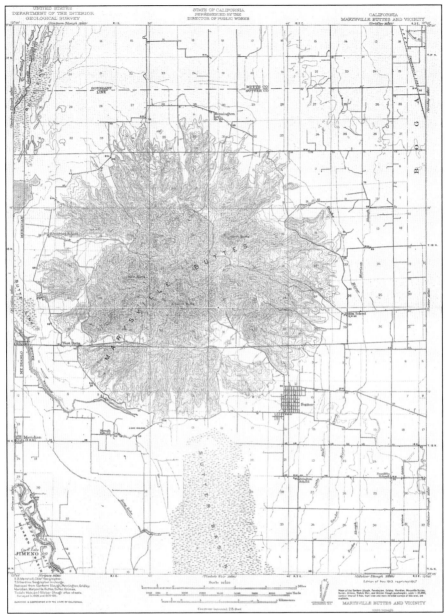

The U.S. Geological Survey (USGS) printed a small-scale topographic map of the Marysville Buttes in 1913 and updated it in 1947. With standard 7.5-minute scale topographical maps, one would have to assemble six maps to have the complete view that this scale provided. It has not been printed for years. (MMF.)

ON THE COVER: Photographer Billy McMurtry brought his Kodak folding camera up South Butte to capture this rest stop halfway to the summit on a blustery spring day. The "fairer sex" in their Sunday finery were happy to sit for this photograph, taken around 1920, to catch their breath. The guys, dressed in ties and sport coats and carrying walking staffs, stood still just long enough for the shutter to click. Those in the group are not named but all appear to be 16 to 18 years old. (Brian McMurtry.)

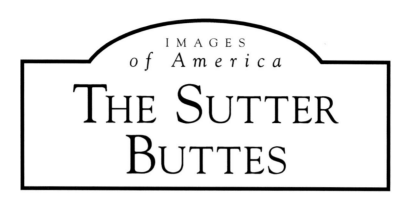

IMAGES
of America

THE SUTTER BUTTES

Michael Don Hubbartt

ARCADIA
PUBLISHING

Published by Arcadia Publishing
Charleston, South Carolina

Printed in the United States of America

Library of Congress Control Number: 2009935205

For all general information contact Arcadia Publishing at:
Telephone 843-853-2070
Fax 843-853-0044
E-mail sales@arcadiapublishing.com
For customer service and orders:
Toll-Free 1-888-313-2665

Visit us on the Internet at www.arcadiapublishing.com

To the Landowners of the Sutter Buttes
Past, Present, and Future
Whose lives, farms, and ranches have preserved a historic landscape

CONTENTS

Acknowledgments   6

Introduction   7

1.   Mapping the World's Smallest Mountain Range   9

2.   Spirit Mountain   25

3.   Discovery of a New Land   41

4.   Pioneers and Settlers   51

5.   Buttes Families   65

6.   Towns Around the Buttes   87

7.   Farms and Ranches   113

ACKNOWLEDGMENTS

I wish to express my gratitude to the families who live and work around the Sutter Buttes, especially to those who opened up their homes and allowed me to leaf through their photograph albums and scrapbooks. That has been the most gratifying aspect of this project. My presence here in the shadow of the Buttes is but 30 years, just one generation. Their families have been here four, five, and even six generations. I did not connect with some families, but in our meetings and exchanges over the years, we have shared common experiences and an unspoken sentiment about the Buttes. This has also contributed much to my understanding of what the Buttes mean to all of us. That is the impetus for this project.

To Julie Stark and Sharyl Simmons and the Community Memorial Museum of Sutter County (CMMSC) volunteer staff: I am thankful for the opportunity and trust to access your archival files and photographs again and again. And also to Gina Zurakowski and the Yuba County Library California Room Collection (YCLCR). Many thanks to the California State University, Chico Meriam Library Special Collections staff; and to the helpful staff at the California State Historical Library. I am grateful for my association with colleagues and friends at California State Parks that has provided me a casual social access to many specialists who shared their thoughts, perspectives, and encouragement.

Local historians are both inspiring and intimidating. To Louise Butts Hendrix, Don Burtis, and Dorothy Jenkins Ross: I now have such respect and appreciation for your research and accomplishments! The naturalists, researchers, and professors whom I have worked with in and around the Buttes are for me an amalgam of colleague, mentor, and teacher; such as Walt Anderson, Ira Heinrich, Brian Hausback, and John Cowan. As with the historians, we build on each other's work. I am appreciative to all the guides and directors of the Middle Mountain Foundation (MMF) and to the Sutter County Historical Society members who expressed support and assistance; you are too numerous to list by name.

I am obliged to the many individuals who assisted by making connections, offering ideas, referrals, promotional planning, and even running errands to facilitate this project, thank you. Especially to James and Kara Davis of Amicus Books for getting me started and to Anne Adams for your objective counsel and patient, affectionate ear. My thanks, also, to Arcadia editors Kelly Reed, Devon Weston, and Sabrina Heise for their positive encouragement and technical assistance to keep me on track.

I am pleased to express my special gratitude for the support of my mother, Barbara Hubbartt Gruening, her husband Dewert, my twin brother Bill, and to Marlene, who expressed her encouragement from afar. I am beholden to Vern Hill, who led me to the top of North Butte 30 years ago, and especially to Karen Morrison without whose computer wizardry and editorial input, I could not have assembled this work! I thank you all.

INTRODUCTION

Situated just 50 miles north of Sacramento, California, in the midst of miles and miles of manicured farmland, the Sutter Buttes appear to be a mountainous island, oddly out of place and time. That prominence on the horizon offers a sense of home and reassuring permanence in a fast-paced, changing world to those who live around the Buttes, from Meridian to Live Oak to Gridley, and from Colusa to Yuba City.

The surprising silhouette of this small mountain range in the middle of a broad agricultural valley provokes the interest and curiosity of motorists traveling the highways. Its prominence makes it a landmark in every sense of the word today as it has throughout California's history. It was a refuge for trappers and explorers from the high waters when the winter rains caused the nearby rivers to overflow. It was the northern border for John Sutter's land grant and later a sentinel and a staging ground for the military during the unsettling times leading up to the Bear Flag Revolt. After California was added to the Union and county lines were drawn, the Buttes were briefly within Butte County and became its namesake.

At a 2,100-foot elevation, the highest peak in the 10-mile range barely meets the geologists' criteria to be a mountain. Its diminutive volcanic stature cannot compare to the grandeur of Mount Shasta or Mount Lassen or the majesty of Yosemite Valley, but its allure lies in its centralized accessibility, its anomalous character, and its serene numinous presence. It has attracted humanity throughout the ages.

For centuries native Patwin and Maidu Indians revered this landform. Some accounts convey that they believed that when Earth-maker created the world, it was here that the first man and woman were created, and that the souls of the departed ascended into heaven at the Buttes.

These native peoples, who lived for centuries in the proximity of these peaks, identified them with words that we translate to mean "Spirit Mountain" or the "Middle Mountain." Anthropologists endeavoring to learn and record their native tongue discovered that this landform was unclaimed and not a place of permanent inhabitation, but rather a gathering place, as evidenced by numerous bedrock milling sites for acorn preparation. Native people to the west were identified as Patwin or Southern Wintun. Their word for this place was *Onolaitotl*. To the northeast were the Maidu, whose names for the Buttes the anthropologists set down on paper phonetically pronounced *Histum Yani*, while in the dialect of related southern Maidu or Nisenan tribal groups to the southeast the name was pronounced *Esto Yamani*. Though spellings of these spoken languages may vary, the spiritual significance of that mountain to these people did not.

The Buttes, first explored by Europeans during the first half of the 19th century, were noted on maps and offered a point of orientation for travelers up and down the broad Sacramento Valley. The name for this landmark has changed over the years as control of the land moved from culture to culture, and from territory to province to nation.

The Spanish moved into California in the late 1700s, reaching the present Sacramento Valley in the early 1800s. Their maps identified the small conspicuous cluster of peaks *Los Picachos* and later as *Los Tres Picos*. In 1833, Hudson Bay trappers led by John Work made their way south from the Pacific Northwest. His journal names the site of their encampment as *Bute Mountain*. Documents that chronicle the increasing Anglo settlements that led up to the Gold Rush, California's statehood in 1850, and up through the beginning of the 20th century record various forms of this appellation—the Sacramento Buttes, the Marysville Buttes, and the Sutter Buttes. It was not until 1949 that the designation Sutter Buttes was made official.

The Buttes have been written about extensively over the past 150 years in journals, memoirs, newspapers, periodicals, books, and scientific studies. The first goal of this pictorial history publication was to collect this diverse assortment of articles by peeking into trappers', explorers', and military journal entries; examining the details of old lithographs that were prevalent before the advent of photography; reading the descriptions and noting their prejudicial depiction of Native Americans. Subsequent articles described the growth of farms and towns around the Buttes.

Old maps of this period reveal the names of early Buttes' landowners. The significance of this fact is that many of the descendents of these families still maintain ranching and farming operations in and around the Sutter Buttes today. Their family businesses impact the land minimally, thus preserving much of the Buttes' historic legacy. We invite you to leaf through old photographs from their scrapbooks and photograph albums and read a synopsis of their words and stories as handed down to their descendents today.

As you peruse the history of the Sutter Buttes, take in the details of the old photographs and you will be drawn to the faces of the people. Unlike names carved on tombstones in area cemeteries, you will begin to connect with these individuals as their personalities and emotions emerge, and perhaps you will begin to feel as they do, a connection to this landscape that transcends more than just a source of income. That feeling prevails among those who live, work, and play in and around the Sutter Buttes today.

A vestige of California's past, the Sutter Buttes is still a region of simple pleasure and quietness. It is a place for people to reconnect with the beauty of the natural world, to discover the values of past cultures, to appreciate the industry of the Buttes forefathers, and to reflect upon modern societies' impact on the environment. This book provides an opportunity to connect with the history of a rural community, its people, and a unique landmark that retains an arcadian lure.

One

MAPPING THE WORLD'S SMALLEST MOUNTAIN RANGE

Maps are usually thought of as a tool that aids in finding locations. Numerous central valley area maps collected here date way back and vary significantly. These maps provide more information about society and its values and attitudes towards the landscape at the time they were published, than finding locations.

Early California maps of the European explorers during the first half of the 1800s revealed the expansive swamplands and prominent peaks and ridges, not paths or trails, as there were none. Subsequent maps reveal settlements and routes amid the significant landmarks. Scale and dimension were relative and secondary to proximity. As the land was partitioned and farmed by the late 1800s, parcels were delineated by property lines. By 1900, maps began to convey a proportion and scale that detailed all elements of the land and its usage by man.

Travelers making their way up and down the Sacramento Valley with or without maps have puzzled over the isolation, the incongruity, and the formation of the Butte Mountains or the Marysville Buttes, as they were later identified. This object of curiosity soon became an object of study as scientists began to explore the mountains. Early assessments dating back to the U.S. Navy Exploring Expedition of 1841 concluded it was the remains of volcanic eruption. The volcanic structure of the Buttes was mapped in the early 20th century and this study continues today. It is only in the last 30 years that we have called the Buttes the world's smallest mountain range.

The driving force of economic development has speeded up the tedious step-by-step ascent of academic research. Commercial investments in refined technology pay off in dividends for shareholder profits, but academia also benefits by hitching a ride and tapping into that well of knowledge. Mapping is now underground and performed using satellites. In the Buttes, by maintaining a partnership and dialog with gas and oil companies, there is increased corporate awareness to be sensitive and protect our beautiful environmental heritage.

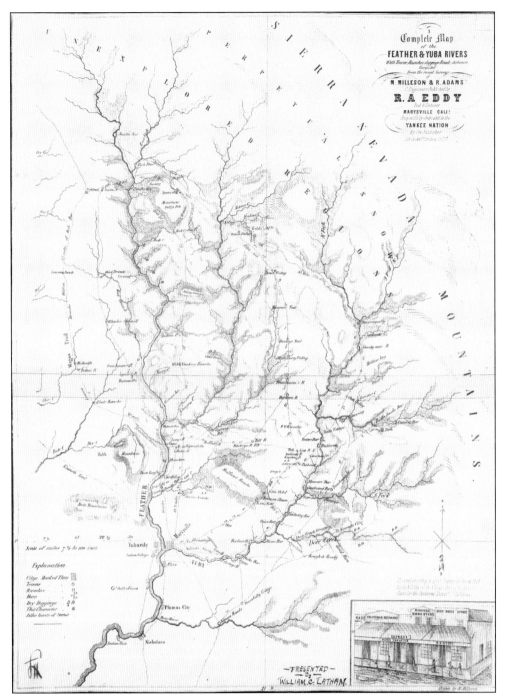

The R. A. Eddy map of 1851 depicts the gold regions of the Sierra Nevada. While scale and proximity of some of the features like Table Mountain are skewed, the map offers a window into significant features and place names of the era. The prominence of the "Bute" Mountains warrants their inclusion as a landmark. They are pictured in this map as having an elongated appearance, due to the southern exposure, causing them appear to stretch out from east to west. That perception is still often repeated by many people today. (YCLCR.)

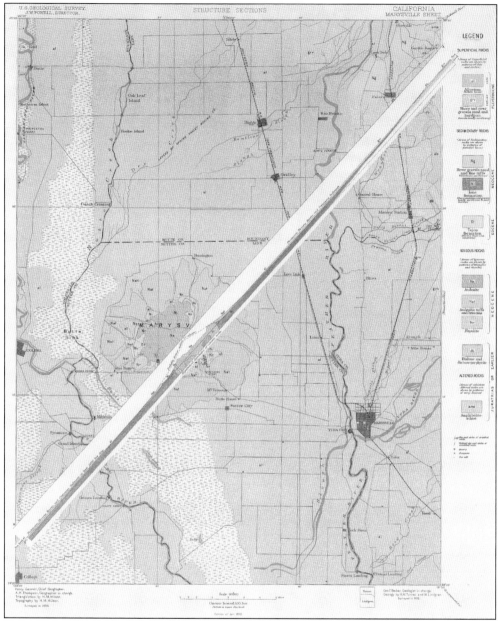

H. M. Wilson completed the triangulation and topography of the U.S. Geological survey for the Sutter Buttes area in 1886, and Turner and Lingren surveyed the geology in 1892. This map was published as part of a folio in 1895. It was one of the resources available to a young geologist who would soon initiate a research project there. Note the cross section of the Buttes depicting the "probable former altitude of volcano." (YCLCR.)

Student of U.C. Declares Buttes Are Old Volcano

ummit Now 2100 Feet High Called Core of Long Extinct Peak.

BERKELEY, Dec. 2.—A brand ew variety of skeleton has been iscovered in California.

While other scientists are busy nearthing and cataloging the keletons of prehistoric men and ncient mammals, Howel Williams, raduate student at the University California, devotes his time to ie study of the remains of an exnct volcano.

The "skeleton," better known the public as the Marysville uttes, is of volcanic origin, acording to Williams, and the peak ow visible, 2100 feet high, is the plug" or core of the original volano, composed of solidified lava.

"The volcano never erupted lava a liquid form," declares Wilams. "Evidently the core of lava elled up from the interior of the arth without sufficient force to ow over the country, and then, fter this core solidified, plugging p the hole, a great explosion took lace, blowing ashes and hard lava or miles around."

The core itself was found to be aree or four miles in diameter by illiams, while the lip of ash, coresponding to a crater, is about n miles across.

The Marysville Buttes, about ten iles west of Marysville, are the rst to be attacked by Williams nce his arrival here on a traveling llowship from the Imperial Colge of Science and Technology, ondon. Williams plans to study l the volcanoes in America.

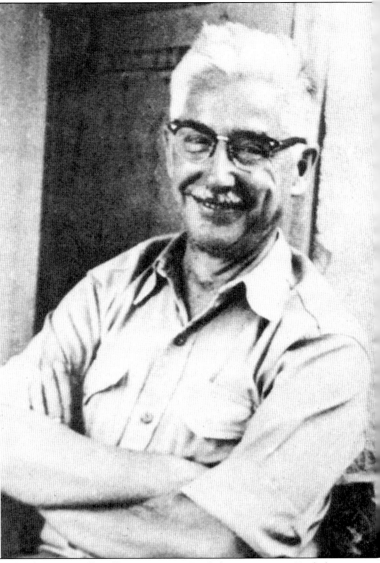

With degrees in geography and archeology, Howell Williams, a young Englishman, came to Berkeley on a three-year appointment as a Commonwealth Fund fellow to study geology. His fieldwork took him to the Marysville Buttes. There he compiled a study of the origins of the oddly situated range that drew the attention of professional colleagues as well as the media. This undated news clipping probably appeared concurrently with the publication of his study in 1928. Williams, pictured later in life, came to be regarded as an eminent volcanologist. (CMMSC.)

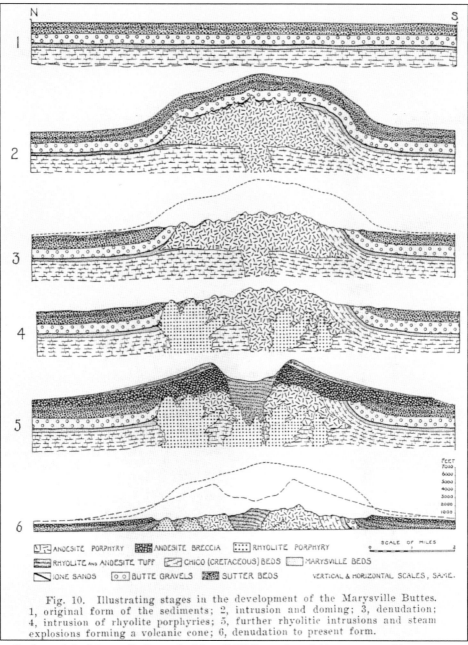

Fig. 10. Illustrating stages in the development of the Marysville Buttes. 1, original form of the sediments; 2, intrusion and doming; 3, denudation; 4, intrusion of rhyolite porphyries; 5, further rhyolitic intrusions and steam explosions forming a volcanic cone; 6, denudation to present form.

The Geology of the Marysville Buttes by Howell Williams listed 41 resource publications, and it included 35 maps, diagrams, and photographs. This series of cross sections reveals Williams's theory of the mountain's growth and deformation. He postulated the Buttes' eruption pushed the surface up to exceed a 5,000-foot elevation. Drawing from observations at recent volcanic eruptions, his study was so thoroughly documented and researched that he received instant recognition from the Geological Society of America for having contributed the "most important paper setting forth the results of his own research in geology." Later studies disprove the old theory of this volcano dome rising to a 5,000-foot elevation. (*Geology of the Maryville Buttes*, donated by Dr. Everett Lindsay.)

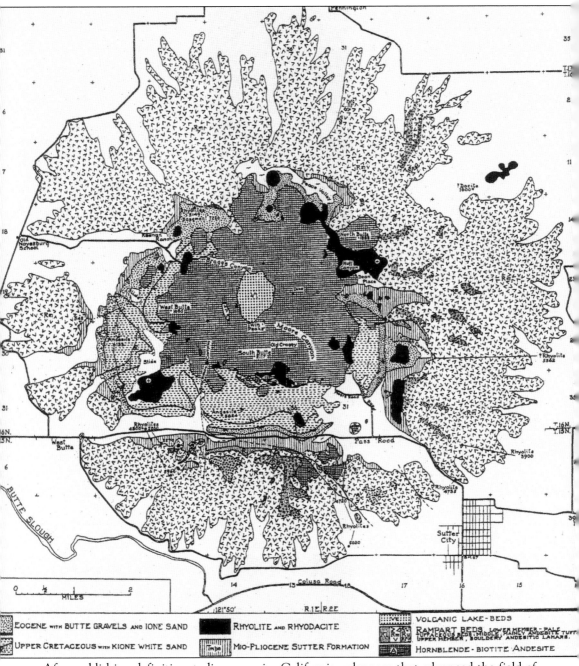

EOCENE with BUTTE GRAVELS and IONE SAND   RHYOLITE and RHYODACITE   VOLCANIC LAKE-BEDS

UPPER CRETACEOUS with KIONE WHITE SAND   MIO-PLIOCENE SUTTER FORMATION

RAMPART BEDS, LOWER MEMBER - PALE TUFFACEOUS BEDS; MIDDLE, FLIMSY ANDESITE TUFF; UPPER MEMBER, BOULDERY ANDESITIC LAHARS.

HORNBLENDE - BIOTITE ANDESITE

After publishing definitive studies on major California volcanoes that advanced the field of volcanological research and as a professor who has been described as the father of volcanology, Willie—as he was known in his field— returned to the Sutter Buttes in the late 1970s to, as stated in *Sutter Buttes of California: A Study of Plio-Pleistocene Volcanism*, "correct the mistakes I made there half a century ago." The advent of gas well drilling profiles and radiometric potassium-argon dating had opened up new techniques for gathering and refining data. (*The Sutter Buttes of California: A Study of Plio-Pleistocene Volcanism*, by Howell Williams and G. H. Curtis.)

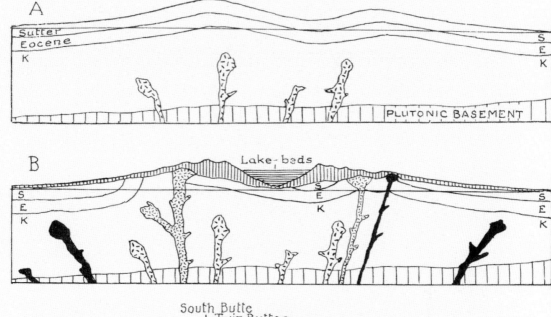

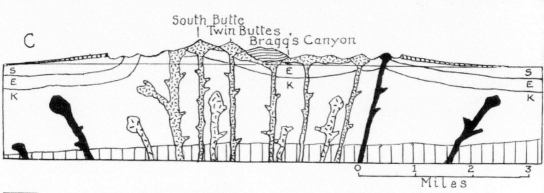

Collaborating with Garniss Curtis, Willie re-evaluated his original work. Scientific rock dating verified the oldest igneous formations to be rhyolite domes, shown here (and on the previous map) in black. The central peaks that make up the Buttes distinctive silhouette are in the inner core of younger and higher jagged peaks of andesite. Multiple extrusions took place over hundreds of thousands of years. A central lake bed once filled up with 1,000 feet of detritus. (*The Sutter Buttes of California*, by Howell Williams and G. H. Curtis.)

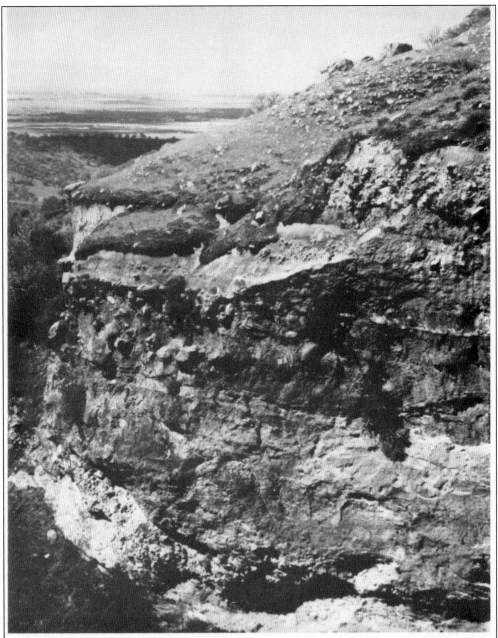

6b. Rampart beds on the northwest side of the buttes. Whitish beds at the base belong to the basal, rhyolite-rich member; overlying beds of the middle member consist chiefly of waterlaid andesitic debris

Eons of rainy, stormy weather impacting the landscape causes erosion, slumping, washouts, and collapses that occur constantly in mountainous terrain. Water sculpts the landscape, exposing layers of the geologic formation below the surface. Williams documented his study with photographs like this one of a deep gully that readily reveals the Buttes' stratified volcanic structure. (*The Sutter Buttes of California,* by Howell Williams and G. H. Curtis.)

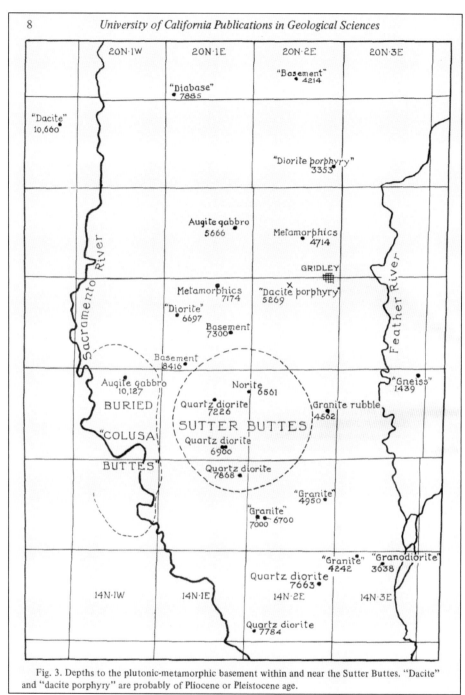

Fig. 3. Depths to the plutonic-metamorphic basement within and near the Sutter Buttes. "Dacite" and "dacite porphyry" are probably of Pliocene or Pleistocene age.

The numbers on this map represent the depth of the bedrock basement beneath the alluvial valley floor around the Sutter Buttes. Under and near the town of Colusa—5 miles to the west—gas well drillers were surprised to discover subterranean domes of rhyolite, some 1,500 feet above the surrounding basement floor, which are called the buried Colusa Buttes. Though not annotated on this map, the town of Colusa is situated at the underside of the Sacramento River opposite the word "Colusa." (*The Sutter Buttes of California,* by Howell Williams and G. H. Curtis.)

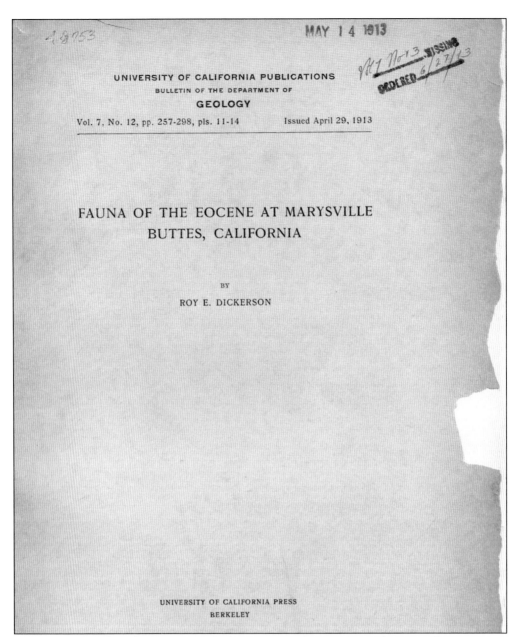

MAY 14 1913

UNIVERSITY OF CALIFORNIA PUBLICATIONS
BULLETIN OF THE DEPARTMENT OF
GEOLOGY
Vol. 7, No. 12, pp. 257-298, pls. 11-14   Issued April 29, 1913

FAUNA OF THE EOCENE AT MARYSVILLE
BUTTES, CALIFORNIA

BY

ROY E. DICKERSON

UNIVERSITY OF CALIFORNIA PRESS
BERKELEY

In laymen's terms the title means animals characteristic of a region, period, or special environment from a geological epoch of approximately 56 to 34 million years ago in the Marysville Buttes. The volcanic intrusion of the Buttes bends upward deeply buried layers that reveal the earth's geologic and biologic history. The stratum becomes exposed from erosion, revealing the remains of life forms that confirm the presence of California's ancient inland sea. (*Fauna of the Eocene at Marysville Buttes*, by Roy E. Dickerson, donated by Geoff Kauffman.)

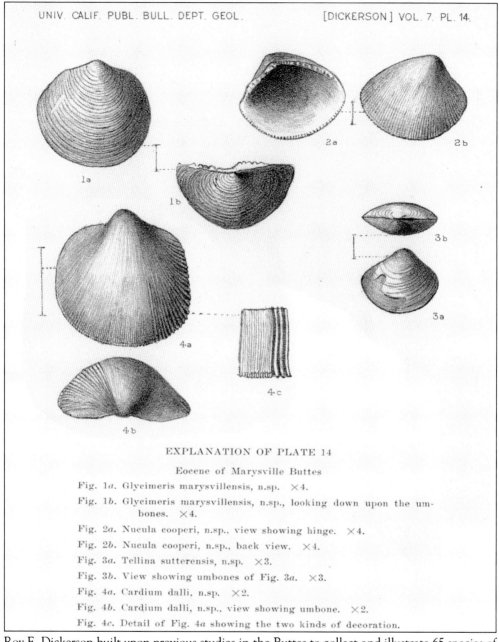

EXPLANATION OF PLATE 14

Eocene of Marysville Buttes

Fig. 1*a*. Glycimeris marysvillensis, n.sp. ×4.

Fig. 1*b*. Glycimeris marysvillensis, n.sp., looking down upon the umbones. ×4.

Fig. 2*a*. Nucula cooperi, n.sp., view showing hinge. ×4.

Fig. 2*b*. Nucula cooperi, n.sp., back view. ×4.

Fig. 3*a*. Tellina sutterensis, n.sp. ×3.

Fig. 3*b*. View showing umbones of Fig. 3*a*. ×3.

Fig. 4*a*. Cardium dalli, n.sp. ×2.

Fig. 4*b*. Cardium dalli, n.sp., view showing umbone. ×2.

Fig. 4*c*. Detail of Fig. 4*a* showing the two kinds of decoration.

Roy E. Dickerson built upon previous studies in the Buttes to collect and illustrate 65 species of seashells at several sites in the Buttes. The actual sizes of the specimens were shown with the adjoining scale that accompanies each drawing. The largest shell depicted here was about three-fourths of an inch. When corroborated with other studies, these findings enable researchers to deduce water depth, climatic conditions, and geologic time periods. (*Fauna of the Eocene at Marysville Buttes*, by Roy E. Dickerson, donated by Geoff Kauffman.)

19

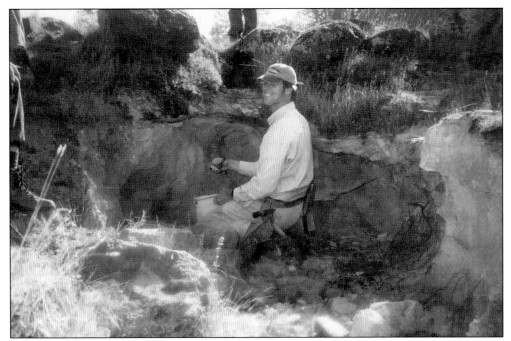

A million and a half years of geological history are evident to volcanologist Brian Hausback, who has been studying the Sutter Buttes since 1988. Roads cut, a quarry excavation, or an eroded drainage, as pictured here, offer close examination of the layered structure of the Sutter Buttes volcano. A newly exposed Ione sands layer, once beneath the valley floor, provided a delightfully unanticipated opportunity for inspection. (K. Morrison.)

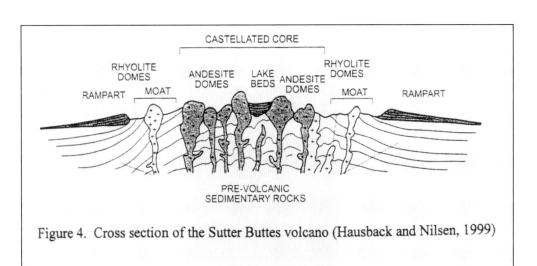

Figure 4. Cross section of the Sutter Buttes volcano (Hausback and Nilsen, 1999)

Williams and Curtis's work described the Sutter Buttes volcano using a castle metaphor. Its distinctive peaks were called the castellated core, like the high towers in the citadel's center. Its peripheral circular valleys, a moat, and the radiating ridges extending outward, ramparts. Drawing from the Williams-Curtis study, Hausback created this volcanic cross section to illustrate the Buttes' geologic formation using the castle nomenclature. (Hausback and Nilsen.)

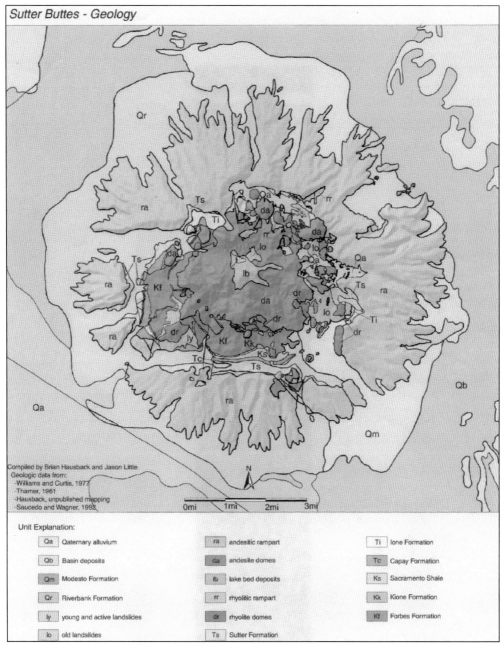

Sutter Buttes - Geology

Compiled by Brian Hausback and Jason Little
Geologic data from:
-Williams and Curtis, 1977
-Thamer, 1961
-Hausback, unpublished mapping
-Saucedo and Wagner, 1992

0mi   1mi   2mi   3mi

Unit Explanation:

Qa	Qaternary alluvium
Qb	Basin deposits
Qm	Modesto Formation
Qr	Riverbank Formation
ly	young and active landslides
lo	old landslides

ra	andesitic rampart
da	andesite domes
lb	lake bed deposits
rr	rhyolitic rampart
dr	rhyolite domes
Ts	Sutter Formation

Ti	Ione Formation
Tc	Capay Formation
Ks	Sacramento Shale
Kk	Kione Formation
Kf	Forbes Formation

Hausback's research has refined our understanding of Buttes' volcanic origins. In the 1990s, the eruptions were dated to have occurred between 1.59 and 1.36 million years ago, reaching heights just over the 2,100-foot elevation, slightly higher than they are today. He offers reassurances regarding the current volcanic status of the Sutter Buttes volcano. Determining it to be inactive, dormant, or extinct is based upon the presence of earthquakes and thermal features such as hot springs or fumaroles. The complete lack of such evidence suggests that there is no molten rock below. It appears to be extinct. Yet research is an ongoing process; like geology, there is always more digging to do. (Brian Hausback and Jason Little.)

21

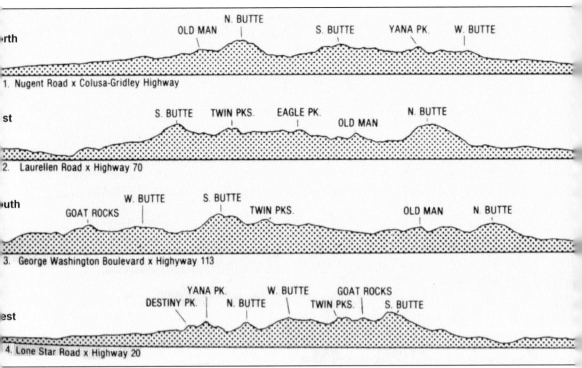

North, south, east, and west: the mountain looks different from each direction. Residents of each town around the Buttes feel a proprietary connection to their perspective of the diminutive range of peaks: Gridley from the north, Colusa from the west, Sacramento from the south, Yuba City and Live Oak from the east. "They are *Our* Buttes," local residents boast. (*The Sutter Buttes, A Naturalist View* by Walt Anderson.)

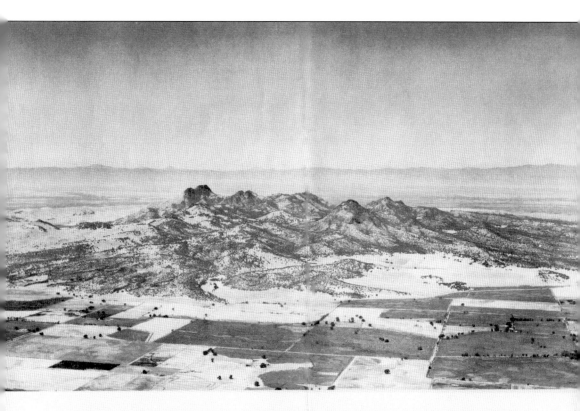

View west toward Sutter Buttes, an eroded inactive Pliocene volcano, which pierces the flat alluvial plain of the Sacramento Valley and stands as a prominent landmark 10 miles in diameter and 2100 feet above the valley floor. A central crater filled with vent tuff lies within an andesite porphyry core. Surrounding the steep-sided and craggy core is a ring of rounded hills composed of folded and faulted Cretaceous, Eocene, and early Pliocene sedimentary beds. These beds in turn are girdled by an outer ring of andesite tuff which forms long gentle ridges that merge into the valley alluvium. Scattered through the sedimentary beds and central core are later intrusions of rhyolite porphyry.

Photo by Clyde Sunderland, Oakland

The Resources Agency of the State of California published this Chico sheet of the geologic map of California dated 1962, which catalogs geology research and provides charts and maps for orientation. It featured this aerial image of the Sutter Buttes with a brief description of their volcanic origin. Note the photograph's caption (with a magnifying glass). Without the benefit of modern rock-dating technology, the caption misidentifies the sequence of rhyolite intrusions, which actually preceded the andesitic activity. (Dorothy Jenkins Ross.)

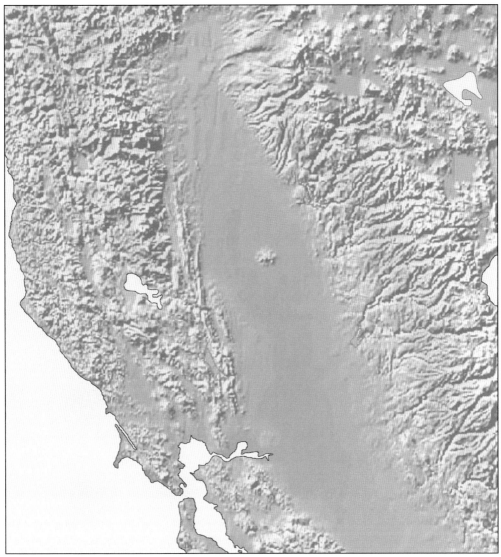

A computer-enhanced image of California's Sacramento Valley accentuates the timeless geologic features of the Golden State, uncluttered by the enterprise of modern man. Our eyes are at once drawn to the solitary protrusion in the center, which reveals the diminutive scale and isolation of the Sutter Buttes in contrast to the surrounding coast and Sierra Nevada mountain ranges. No wonder it is promoted locally as "the World's Smallest Mountain Range." But would we not have to catalog all of them to verify that assertion? (Ron Ross, from *The Blue Oak* by Dorothy Jenkins Ross.)

Two

Spirit Mountain

Thousands of years before the European explorers made forays into the area we now call California, indigenous people thrived in a landscape that was rich in natural resources. So abundant and diverse was the wildlife and vegetation that much of California supported a greater density of natives than the rest of the North American continent above Mexico.

Most of our U.S. history, until recently, focused upon America's westward expansion, the discovery of gold, and the opportunity to develop an unexplored land. Moving west across the country, pioneers encountered many native tribes. The potential for conflict kept everyone on guard with guns ready to fire. To these newcomers, controlling the threat of local natives was as much a part of the movement west as was the threat of wolves or grizzly bears.

The pioneers regarded indigenous people the same as they did most people of color in the mid-1800s, as inferior races. In California, Native Americans were called "diggers," a pejorative voiced with disdain, because they dug up roots with sticks. Strong words, to be sure, but nothing speaks clearer than the words of the writers, journalists, and travelers of the day.

Some of these people recognized the problem and spoke out in their defense, but even they seemed resigned to the notion that the native race was facing the same extinction as the large, dangerous carnivores, or could only be preserved by confining them on distant reservations. Forced relocations of native peoples were effective only in moving their "troublesome" presence elsewhere.

Even those who cared for these displaced people noted behaviors regarded as strange and felt compelled to civilize them or to convert them to our ways. By 1860, according to the *John Sutter* biography by Albert Hurtado, there were only 10 Native Americans in all of Sutter County. Consequently, our study includes images from both the wide Patwin and Maidu tribal areas that surround the Buttes.

The Sutter Buttes have always been revered by the local native societies, yet writings of the period reveal little awareness or sensitivity of such significance until anthropologists and archeologists began to probe beneath the material superficialities of native cultures.

Historical images that depict scenes of these natives likewise tend to reflect an uncomplimentary cultural bias that was not recognized until our modern attitudes began to respect and appreciate cultural diversity.

The Tribes of California

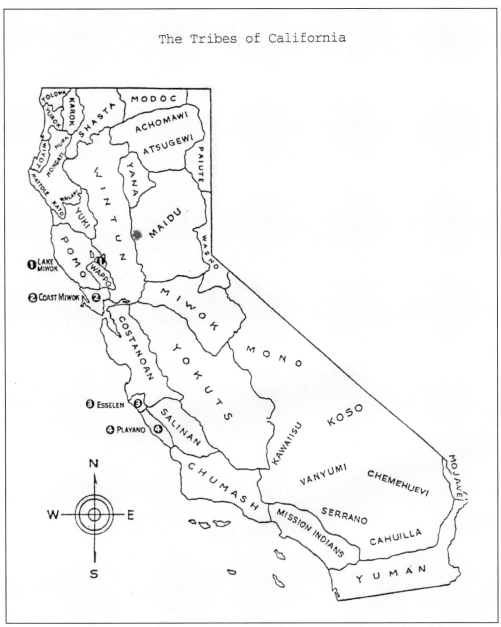

The Buttes are situated near the Sacramento River, which separates the Maidu and the Wintun tribal areas. This statewide map lists 40 territories, but language and cultural diversity, according to some authorities, distinguishes more than 80 tribal entities within California, each as distinctive as the nations of Europe. These people had sophisticated cultures and lived a relaxed, fluid lifestyle that ebbed and flowed with the seasonal blossoming and maturing of vegetation and the migrations of the wildlife, waterfowl, and fish in the rivers and streams. (Prof. David Rubiales.)

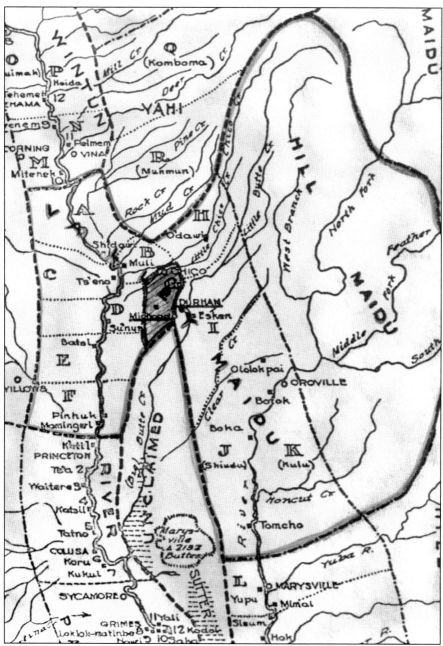

A closer look at the Wintun and Maidu tribal areas reveals numerous village sites along the Sacramento and Feather Rivers. The pioneers called these *rancherias*. Variations in language and cultural practices of these people distinguished tribal affiliation and identification for anthropologists who later studied them. The southern Wintun here are called River Patwin, and the darkened outline delineates the valley and hill Maidu; the shaded area is the Mechoopda Maidu. Note that the area near the Buttes is identified as unclaimed on this map. As anthropologists pieced together an understanding of the native culture in oral interviews, the spiritual significance of the Buttes to all the local tribes became apparent. (CSUC Meriam Library, Dorothy Hill Collection, Sc35154.)

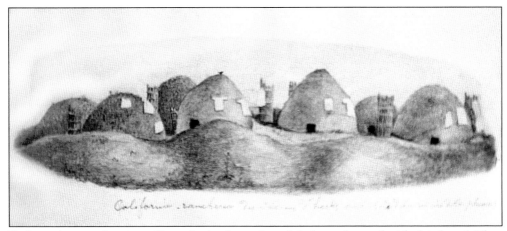

Early renderings of native villages depict dome-shaped shelters plastered with dried mud. They were called *k'um* or *k'umi*. This painting by Fritz Wilkersheim, *c.* 1850, shows a Maidu village identified on old maps as Hok. It was on the Feather River near the site of Sutter's country estate. Note the details such as the cylindrical brush granaries and clothing laid out to dry. (CSUC Meriam Library, Dorothy Hill Collection, Sc30224.)

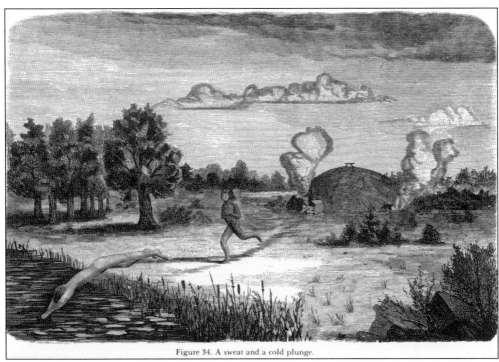

Figure 34. A sweat and a cold plunge.

In the early 1870s, Stephen Powers traveled and lived with California Indians, recording aspects of their lives. His image of a dance house or sweat lodge depicted a practice then regarded as odd. He wrote, "The men often dance with a fantastic violence and persistence until they are reeking with perspiration, and then plunge into the cold water." (Sketch by A.W. Chase, *The Tribes of California*, University of California Press.)

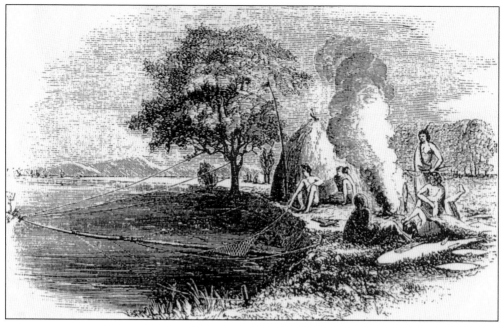

In a Colusa County history published in 1880, Will Green described life among the Native Americans just west of the Buttes: "The river, Butte Creek, and several sloughs were full of fish, and these were caught by means of nets made of wild hemp. . . . Every spring . . . enough [salmon] were caught and dried to last nearly all year." (*Personal Narrative of Explorations* by J.R. Bartlett, courtesy of California State Library.)

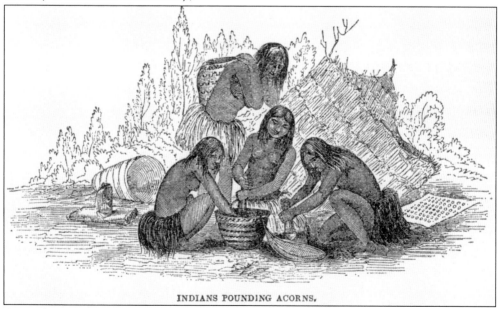

INDIANS POUNDING ACORNS.

An explorer's journal passage describes this scene with judgmental disdain: "Acorns are spread in the sun to dry . . . pounding is performed upon a plank . . . with a stone pestle. . . . This employment presents a busy scene, though the want of cleanliness, I may almost say the pig-like filthiness with which it is performed, excites disgust." (Drawing by Alfred Agate and quote from *Narrative of U.S. Exploring Expedition*, courtesy of Butte County Library.)

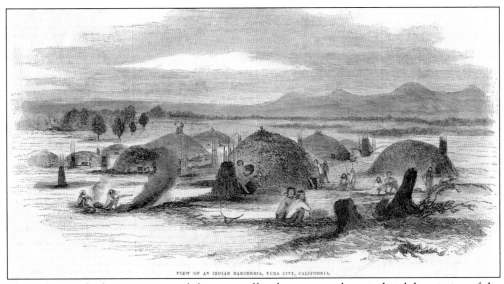

VIEW OF AN INDIAN RANCHERIA, YUBA CITY, CALIFORNIA.

The 1850s article that accompanied this print offered an extremely prejudicial description of the Native American's "filthy and slothful habits." On the same page another writer offered a more respectful perspective, "They can hear more distinctly, see farther, smell clearer, can bear more fatigue, can subsist on less food, and have altogether fewer wants than their white brethren; and yet we consider…red Indians of America as 'outside barbarians.'" (*Gleason's Pictorial Drawing-Room Companion*, courtesy of CMMSC.)

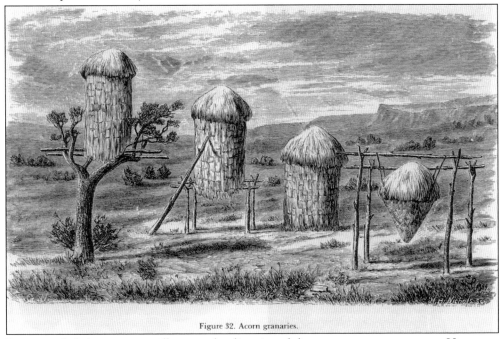

Figure 32. Acorn granaries.

Powers included a picture to illustrate the diversity of the common acorn granary. He wrote, "They wove a cylinder-shaped granary of willow wicker work, three or four feet in diameter and twice as high which they filled with acorns and covered with thatch." Commonly constructed near village sites, he reported that the various forms sometimes were near productive trees, miles away. (*The Tribes of California*, University of California Press)

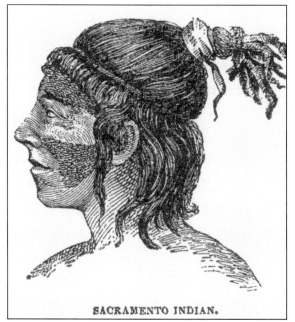

SACRAMENTO INDIAN.

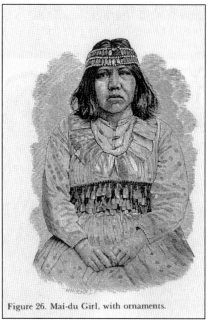

Figure 26. Mai-du Girl, with ornaments.

The Wilkes's Exploring Expedition recorded, "Most of them were naked, others had a piece of deerskin thrown over their shoulders; their faces were marked with an expression of good humour," followed by a description of the hair and tattoos as pictured here. The lithograph on the right illustrates that influences of European settlers brought changes in native lifestyle as well as attire, such as the long dress on the Maidu girl pictured here during the 1870s. Her garment, typical of the settlers' feminine clothing, is adorned with the natives' highly valued abalone shell ornaments. (Upper left, Alfred Agate drawing, Butte County Library; upper right, *The Tribes of California*, University of California Press.)

Accompanying the rancheria lithograph, an article included the description of this pretty dark-skinned girl uncharacteristically depicted with modern jewelry and hair-styling: "Indian women are the patient, laboring, and willing slaves of their lord . . .they do all the domestic drudgery cook, cultivate the few vegetables that are used by the people, do all the household labor, and indeed, carry all the burdens." (*Gleason's Pictorial Drawing Room Companion*, courtesy of CMMSC.)

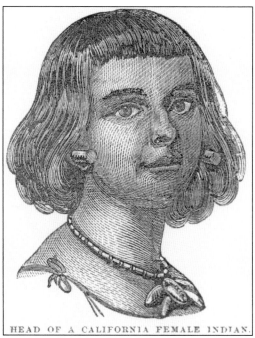

HEAD OF A CALIFORNIA FEMALE INDIAN.

31

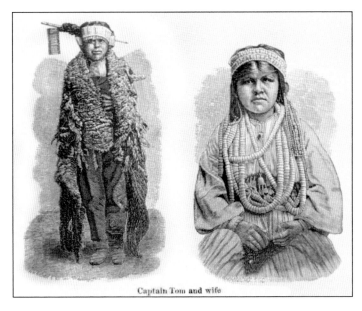

Captain Tom and wife

From the Auburn Nisenan Maidu area, Capt. Tom Lewis and his wife, Jane, display wealth of their culture. His rabbit skin robe could also be used as bedding. His flicker tail headband was usually reserved for ceremonial regalia. Her necklace is hundreds of clamshell beads, carved and drilled like buttons. Their value was such that they were used as currency. (*The Tribes of California*, University of California Press.)

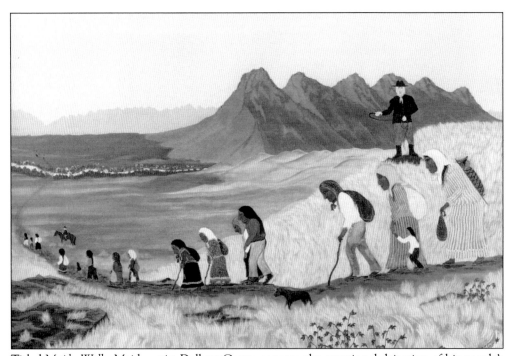

Titled *Maidu Walk*, Maidu artist Dalbert Castro conveys the emotional dejection of his people's forced relocation under armed guard. The scene is more poignant when viewed with the realization that *Esto Yamani*, the Buttes, were for the Maidu a sacred place of deep spiritual significance. Tribal groups were marched from Nevada County and Butte County to Nome Cult Reservation near Round Valley. (Courtesy Dalbert Castro and Aeschliman-McGreal Collection, Oakland Museum.)

MARYSVILLE HERALD.

VOL. I.   MARYSVILLE, YUBA COUNTY, CALIFORNIA, FRIDAY, NOVEMBER 1, 1850.   NO. 26.

The initial issue of this Marysville's first newspaper, appeared August 6, 1850.

The California Gold Rush brought so many miners and settlers into the area that the natural resources that supported the Native American food base were severely depleted, reducing them to poaching or begging for food and even illness or starvation. As public sentiment mounted against this troublesome trend, the daily *Marysville Herald* ran a series of articles between October 14 and December 24, 1856, regarding 66 local Maidu Indians who were rounded up and removed to the Nome Lackee Reservation, 25 miles southwest of Red Bluff. "We have no doubt that it will be in accordance with the wishes of a large majority of this community," wrote the *Marysville Herald*. "They are a wretched set of creatures and their condition in regard to all physical and moral wants is most miserable." (YCLCR.)

33

W. T. Ellis probably represents the best example of people whose lives are committed to improving their community. He was the city's mayor, a county supervisor, and the "father of Marysville's levee system." A small portion of his memoir demonstrates the public attitude of the mid-1800s when it was not unusual to buy a Native American child. (*Memories: My Seventy-Two Years in the Romantic County of Yuba, California*, courtesy of CMMSC.)

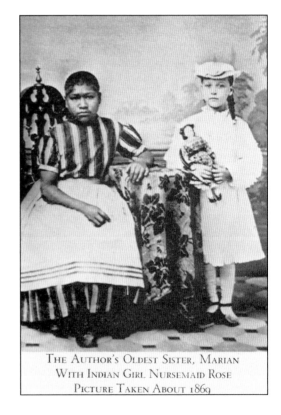

THE AUTHOR'S OLDEST SISTER, MARIAN WITH INDIAN GIRL NURSEMAID ROSE PICTURE TAKEN ABOUT 1869

Ellis wrote, "Shortly after I was born, . . . to look after my elder sister and myself, we had an Indian girl named Rose, who was purchased . . . for $500 . . . she would roll up in a blanket and sleep on the floor . . . she could not stand civilization I guess . . . [after] about 10 years she contracted tuberculosis and died." (*Memories: My Seventy-Two Years in the Romantic County of Yuba, California*, courtesy of CMMSC.)

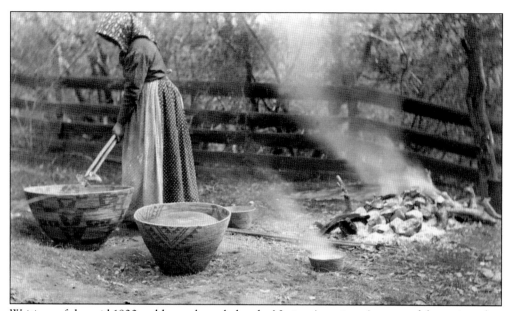

Writings of the mid-1800s seldom acknowledge the Native Americans' resourceful practices that utilized elements of the landscape for utensils and containers. The Maidu woman, here in 1903, is cooking in baskets woven so tightly that they hold water. She is putting a rock from the fire into a large basket full of acorn soup. The rocks hold the heat and boil the soup into a thick porridge. (CSUC Meriam Library, Dorothy Hill Collection Sc31372.)

Basketry fibers were from plants such as split willow and red bud, split conifer roots, maidenhair fern stems, and bear or deer grasses that were tended, cultivated, and harvested seasonally. Each basket's size and shape serves a specific function: cooking or feasting, winnowing or sifting, storage, and even gift baskets. Many of the patterns and designs are symbolic elements of nature. (CSUC Meriam Library, Dorothy Hill Collection, Sc30667.)

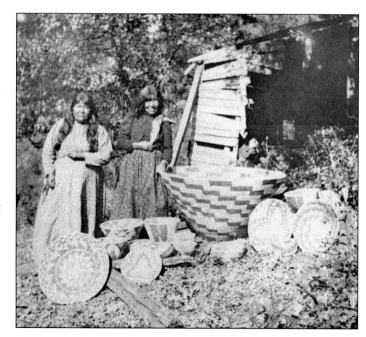

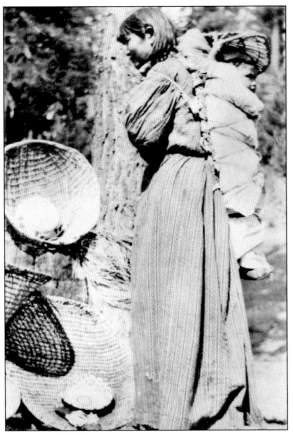

With her child safely tucked in a cradle basket, the Maidu mother in this undated photograph attended to her tasks. The cradle, complete with a sunshade, could be secured to a nearby tree or rock. These specialized carriers were believed to shape or mold the child's character. Some had designs woven in that symbolized desired traits or skills. (CSUC Meriam Library, Dorothy Hill Collection, Sc31358.)

Seasonal gatherings usually centered around ceremonial dances in the round house. Elaborate regalia represented aspects of the natural and spiritual world, and ceremonies, dance steps, rhythm, and chants symbolized a connectedness to nature for sustenance and well-being. Photographed at Cortina in 1925, the Hesi Dance, a renewal celebration for plentiful harvests, may have lasted four days and entreated participants to rejoice and eat together. (CSUC Meriam Library, Dorothy Hill Collection, Sc30930.)

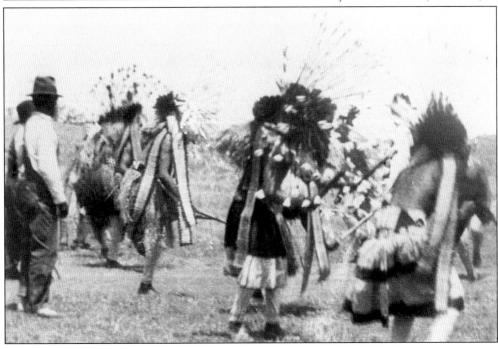

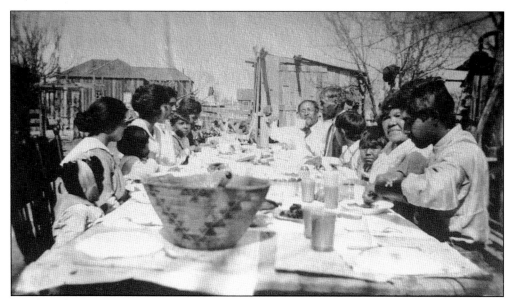

Family gatherings bring three and four generations together to reconnect. The values, skills, and even the language of the old ways live on where tradition and elders are respected. The basket here suggests an unspoken sentiment of native pride and heritage in a more modern time. (CSUC Meriam Library, Dorothy Hill Collection.)

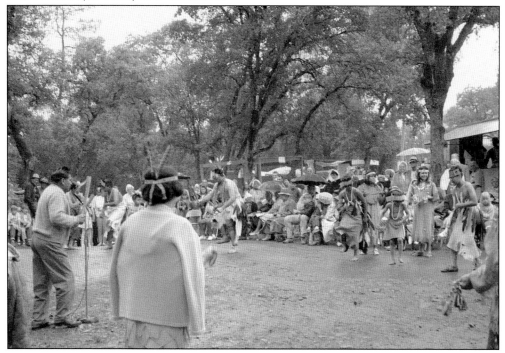

The tradition and significance of ceremonial dances thrives in Patwin and Maidu tribal gatherings today. Big Times gatherings bring together neighboring tribes to celebrate nature's bounty and a shared cultural heritage. Numerous rituals with names like bear, deer, coyote, or duck dance that historically symbolized wildlife encounters are still portrayed. Note the umbrellas—rain does not diminish the fervor of the experience. (CSUC Meriam Library, Dorothy Hill Collection, Sc 30955.)

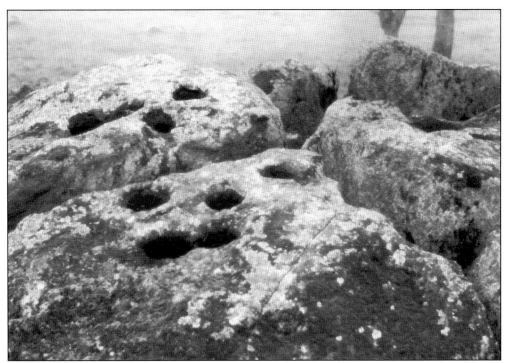

A Maidu kitchen? These boulders have deep grinding holes, indicating repeated usage over the years by native women who pounded acorns into meal. Numerous sites like this are scattered along the drainages between the Buttes sloping ramparts and interior valleys on all four sides of the Buttes. Notably absent are the darkened midden soil and detritus that are indicative of prolonged inhabitation at village sites. (Marlene Hubbartt.)

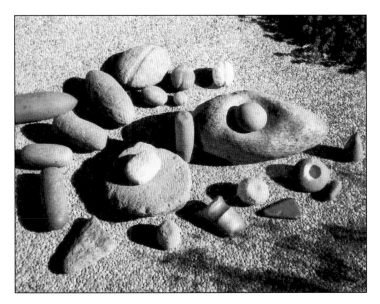

Stones were shaped into a variety of useful implements and tools. The cylindrical pestles were used in the mortar holes to pound the acorns into meal. The round hand stone or mano was used with the portable flattened metate to pulverize small seeds into meal. Round cooking stones, net weights, a hammer or maul, wedges, and charm stones or amulets were shaped by hand. (Dorothy Jenkins Ross.)

Diana Almendariz, of Maidu, Wintun, Hupa, and Yurok descent, teaches the old ways of food preparation, and other Native American skills. "My people used to tell me that women were not allowed to go to the Buttes. It is sacred, they said. But I feel it is my destiny, and at these milling sites where our people used to gather, it feels right." (Hugh Smith.)

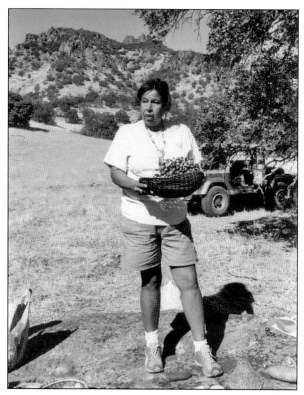

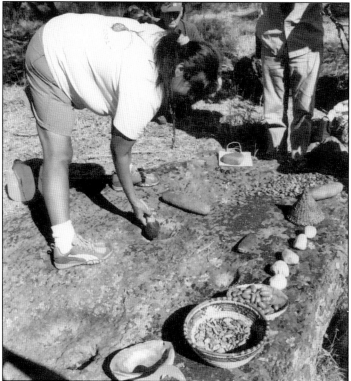

Diana, known as "the Tule lady," uses a soap root brush, handmade out of root fibers, to sweep out a mortar hole prior to demonstrating acorn meal preparation. "The boulder surface hasn't been cared for," she said, "because in olden days it would not be cloaked with mosses—it would be smooth and the holes coated with the oils of our acorns." (Hugh Smith.)

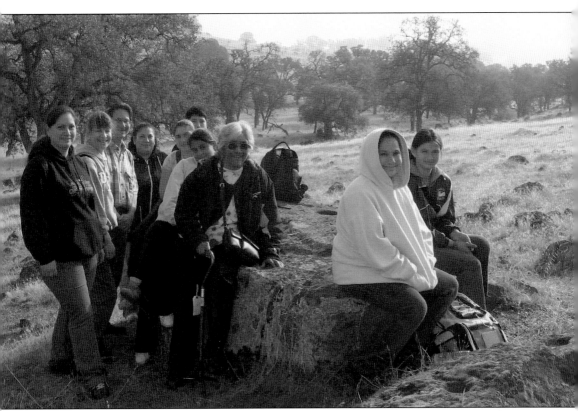

Ren Reynolds of the Enterprise Rancheria in Butte County poses with the Maidu youth group from his tribe at an acorn-milling site on the north side of the Buttes. Grace Delbosque, an elder of the tribe, is at the center of the photograph. Host Ty Shaeffer escorted the group back to the flat-topped boulder that was pocked with six mortar holes, a perfect place to stop for lunch, as their ancestral relations did generations before. (K. Morrison.)

Three

DISCOVERY OF A
NEW LAND

The presence of the Spanish, Russians, and Canadians has been documented on the western frontier in the early 1800s. California was regarded as a land of opportunity where resources were free for the taking. Each nation endeavored to assert their presence and ultimately to acquire this territory with settlements or expeditions. Journals of explorers and trappers from these nations provide for us today with a source of geographic descriptions, weather conditions, and Native American encounters of the time.

Spanish explorer Gabriel Moraga is acknowledged as the first European to have discovered the Sutter Buttes in 1808 during his expedition to scout for new mission sites in California in 1808. In 1821, he was followed by Luis Arguello who commanded a nautical expedition up the rivers. The youthful Jedediah Smith, the first American adventurer, kept an account of his travels near the Buttes in 1828 and recorded Native American encounters

Fur trappers for the Hudson Bay Company based out of Fort Vancouver, near Canada, made regular expeditions into California's central valley. During the rainy winter of 1832–1833, the John Work brigade sought refuge in the Buttes for almost two months from rising waters that surrounded them. After a season of trapping throughout much of central California, he noted in his journal on their way back home that sickness hit his men hard and 61 were ill as they once again made camp in the Buttes.

As part of a worldwide research mission between 1838 and 1842, the Wilkes U.S. Navy Exploring Expedition entered California in 1841 with an assortment of astronomical, meteorological, and surveying instruments, as well as trained scientists, botanists, and even artists to record their findings. The "Sacramento Bute" was of particular interest, as they correctly deduced it to be of volcanic origin.

General Fremont's camp in the Buttes in 1846 has historical significance in relation to the Bear Flag Revolt, which secured independence from Mexico prior to California's annexation to the United States. Subsequent treks into the Buttes, which we have included here, were of a scientific nature. All these expeditions left a legacy of artwork, photographs, and descriptions that contribute to our understanding of California's rich natural and cultural history.

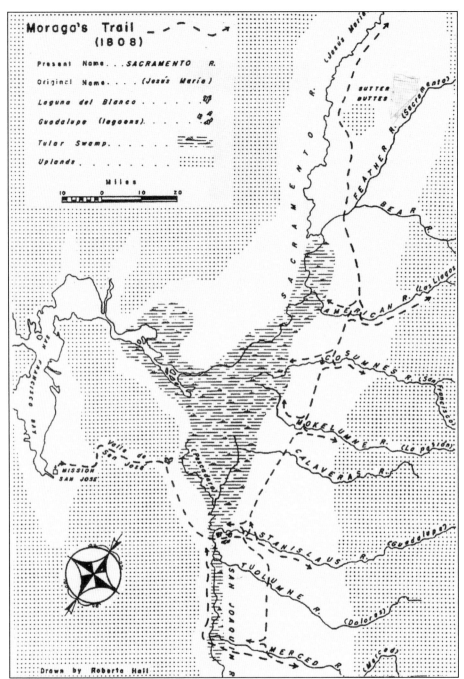

Gabriel Moraga ventured out from Mission San Jose in 1808 to find suitable sites in the central valley for new missions. He describes in his journal a confrontational encounter with Native Americans on October 9, 1808, while fording the Feather River as he made his way towards the Buttes. Thirteen years later Luis Arguello commanded a river expedition to within sight of the Buttes, which he called "Los Pichacos," meaning the peaks, and named a nearby river "Rio de las Plumas," which means river of the feathers, presumably because it was full of floating feathers of numerous waterfowl. (*The Blue Oak*, Dorothy Jenkins Ross.)

Jedediah Smith, an explorer, hunter, and trapper, was the first American to lead a party into Northern California in 1828. A youthful 29-year-old, he was clean-shaven but scarred from a bear attack. A devout Methodist who carried a bible, he nonetheless did not hesitate to use firearms to insure his party's safety. His journal reveals numerous encounters with Native Americans. (Jedediah Smith Society.)

Brigades of trappers from the Hudson Bay Company worked their way down into California. John Work kept journals during the winter of 1832–1833 when his party was stranded in the Buttes due to rising floodwaters. He recorded Native American encounters, the presence of wildlife, and difficulties traveling in the flooded lowlands. This dramatic image from *Memoirs of My Life* by John Fremont captures the essence of that experience. (California History Room, California State Library, Sacramento.)

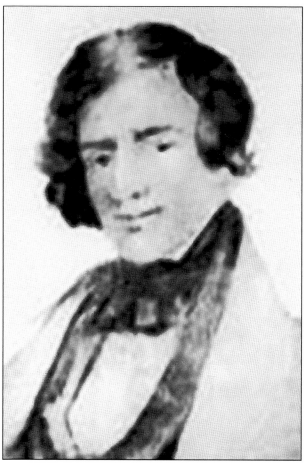

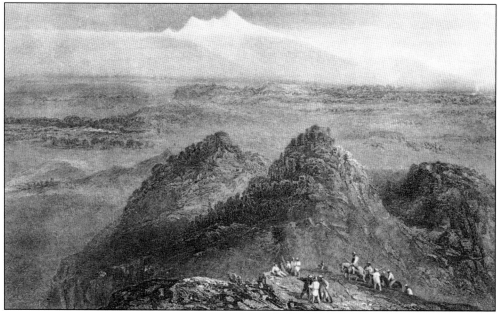

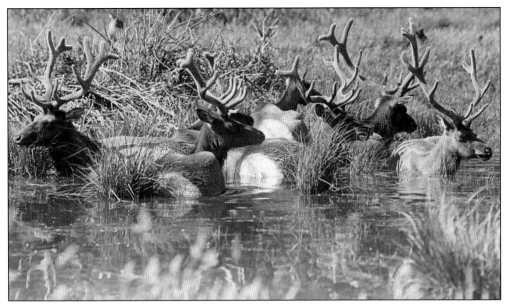

Work's journal reveals that in the course of a month, they killed 395 elk, 148 deer, 17 bears, and 8 antelope. Apparently the game was also confined to the hillsides above the overflowing marshlands. The pictured tule elk were still to be found in central California in the 1920s when this photograph was taken in 1927. (By Joseph Dixon, courtesy of *Jewel in the Pacific Flyway* written by John Cowan.)

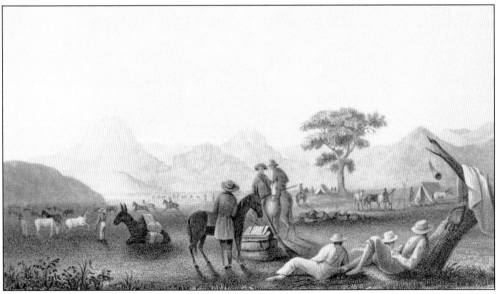

The U.S. Exploring Expedition commanded by Charles Wilkes set out in 1838 to explore and document the distant Pacific islands and the American Northwest wilderness. The assemblage included scientists and artists. In the fall of 1841, a contingent camped near the "Butes" as pictured here. Geologist Thomas Dana ascertained the small mountain range to be an old volcano. (Wilkes' *Narrative of the United States Exploring Expedition*, Butte County Library.)

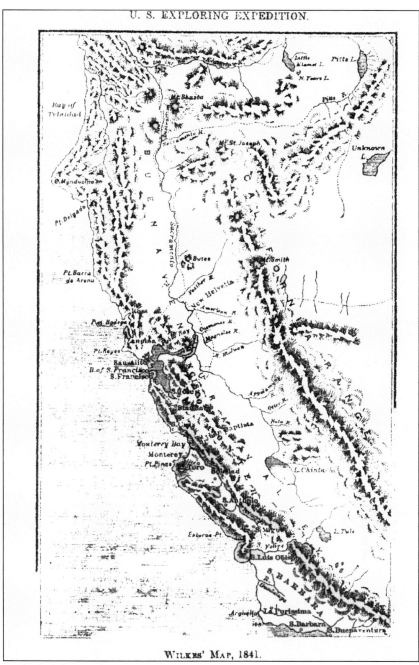

WILKES' MAP, 1841.

The party forded the Feather River near where it joins the Sacramento while heading towards Sutter's Fort at New Helvetia, on their way to rendezvous with Commander Wilkes near Yerba Buena. The diary of midshipman Henry Eld recorded this observation, "On both sides we found a great many skulls and bones of the human bodies that had been buried at the time of the ravage of the fever and ague, which made great havoc among the Indians." Anthropologists have since determined that the sickness that Work's party experienced in 1833 decimated native populations in California's central valley. (Wilkes' *Narrative of the United States Exploring Expedition*, Butte County Library.)

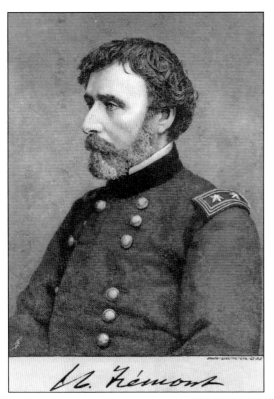

General Fremont, remembered for Bear Flag Revolt, wrote here of other concerns: "My camp in the Buttes became a rendezvous for the settlers. . . . It was evident from the movements of the Indians that the rumored attack on the settlers was certainly intended. . . . I resolved to anticipate the Indians and strike them a blow." (*Memoirs of My Life*, by John Charles Fremont, California History Room, California State Library, Sacramento.)

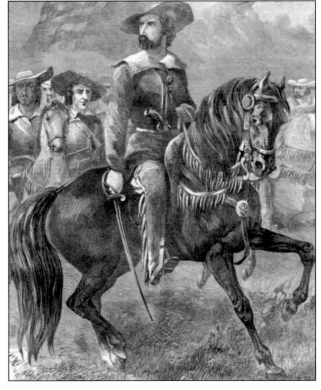

Fremont's memoirs provide his rationale for dealing with the local Native Americans: "Early in the morning I moved quietly out of camp. . . . Intending to surprise and scatter them we rode directly upon them, and . . . several were killed in the dispersion. . . . This was a rude but necessary measure to prevent injury to the whites," as stated in his book *Memoirs of My Life*, California History Room, California State Library, Sacramento. (*Harper's Weekly*.)

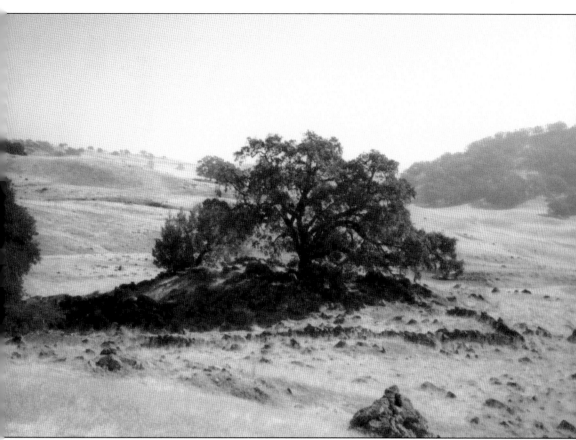

Situated on private property, the Fremont Corral has a stone perimeter, about 3 feet high, which surrounds a huge old oak that would have shaded their mounts 160 years ago. There is still a spring seep nearby. Fremont wrote in his memoirs, "On the 30th [of May 1846] we camped at the Buttes of Sacramento. . . . At our encampment on a small run at the southern base, we were about eight hundred feet above the sea. The mornings were pleasantly cool for a few hours. . . . The hunters always left camp before daylight and were in by nine o'clock, after which the sun grew hot. Game was fat and abundant; upwards of eighty deer, elk, and bear were killed in one morning." (Marlene Hubbartt.)

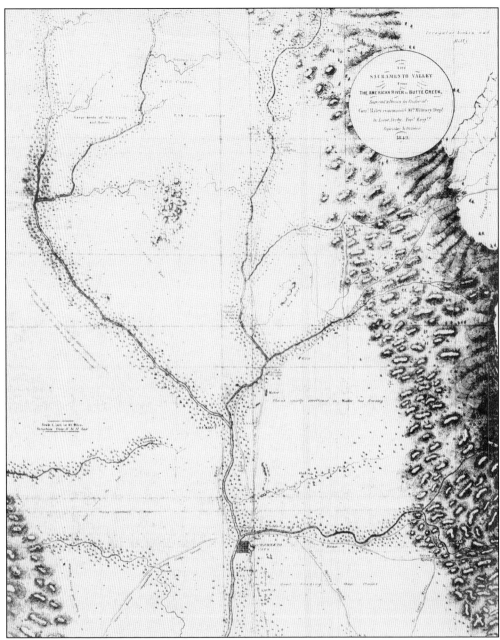

With the advent of the Gold Rush, Lt. George Horatio Derby was commissioned to survey the Sacramento Valley to find an inland site for a fort to protect the miners and settlers. His detailed map here depicts the growth of trees along the waterways, rancheria locations, and notes regarding the abundance of stray livestock and wild elk and antelope grazing on the grasslands. The course of his travels took him around the Buttes, which he described as "presenting a singular spectacle . . . which have been erroneously represented to be three isolated peaks rising in the prairie. They are in reality a range, containing some twenty peaks…" He was particularly fascinated with a "turret-shaped rock 56-feet high" atop the northern butte. (Yolo County Historical Society.)

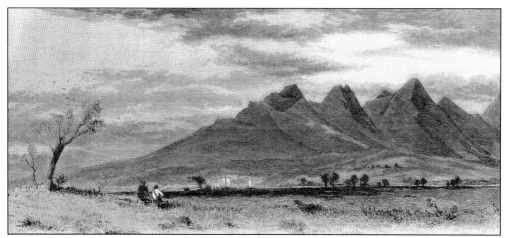

The description of this artistic rendering reads, "The Valley of the Sacramento . . . spreads out into treeless prairies. . . . The first break in the monotony of the expanse is made by the Marysville Buttes—a short range of low volcanic hills. . . . Deep pools here and there give back the blue of the cloudless sky." (*Picturesque America,* or *The Land We Live In,* edited by William Cullen Bryant, 1873.)

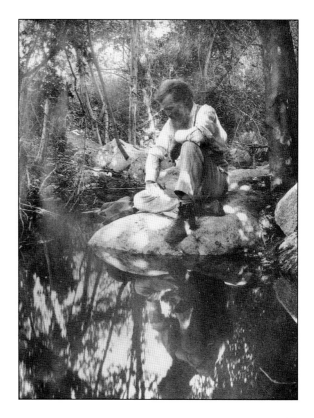

Renowned naturalist and author John Muir was so intrigued by the appearance of the Buttes in October 1877 that he wrote in his journal, "Began to think of climbing a tree to look for the Marysville Buttes, when at the end of a lovely reach, they appeared in full imposing view, exceedingly rugged in outline." (John Muir Papers, Holt-Atherton Special Collections, University of the Pacific Library Copyright 1984 Muir-Hanna Trust.)

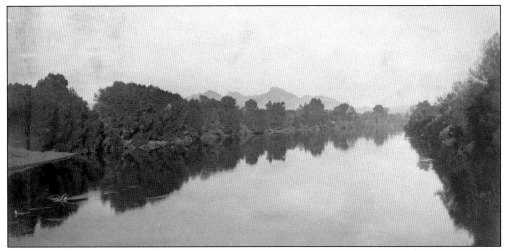

Later, floating down the Sacramento River, John Muir looked back and reflected, "The Buttes for 50 miles or so form a striking feature . . . they loom grandly and effectively as a mountain-range many times higher." This photograph was taken in 1911. (Donna McMaster; Holt-Atherton Special Collections, University of the Pacific Library Copyright 1984 Muir-Hanna Trust.)

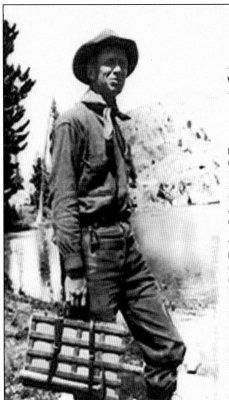

BULLETIN

OF THE

TORREY BOTANICAL CLUB.

Vol. XVIII.]   New York, November 15, 1891.   [No. II.

Botany of the Marysville Buttes.

BY WILLIS L. JEPSON.

Almost in the center of the Sacramento Valley and on the level plain between the two great forks of the Sacramento River, the upper Sacramento and the Feather, lie the Marysville Buttes. Entirely isolated from either the Sierra Nevada or the Coast Range, rising abruptly on every side to a considerable elevation from the level plains, these mountains with their ragged summits and sharp slopes form a striking landmark visible from nearly every portion of the northern Sacramento Valley.

I made my way to the Buttes by means of a river steamer. The banks of the stream were fringed with a dense growth of box elder, oak, willow, cottonwood and sycamore, with a thick undergrowth of *Rubus, Vitis, Sambucus* and *Baccharis.* An occasional break revealed the extensive tule swamps bordering the river for miles, all aglow with great patches of *Cotula.* It was as yet too early to expect much along the river banks and bottoms in the way of annual growths, the winter freshets having only lately receded. But on the plains around Yuba City there was plenty of vegetation and the flora appeared little different from that of the valley sixty miles below; the characteristic spring plants were there in abundance, lupines, clovers, larkspurs, butter-cups, *Brodiæas, Tritelias, Layias, Eschscholtzias, Allocaryas* and *Orthocarpi.* But the moment I reached the Buttes the flora to all appearances changed entirely.

Fresh from Berkeley, young Willis Jepson's *Botany of the Marysville Buttes* provides a clue to the prominent botanical authority he was to become. Here with his plant press, he probably looks much as he did collecting specimens in the Buttes. Willis created an encyclopedic resource, the *Flora of California*, which is still lugged into the Buttes today by serious students of botany. (MMF.)

Four

PIONEERS AND SETTLERS

The historic prominence of John Sutter is evident in the region around the Buttes since the county and mountain bear his name. Yet, we don't find any records to confirm that Sutter even had an interest in them. Although his methods may have been questioned, his accomplishments and his enterprise undoubtedly contributed to opening up the west, and it is this that is recognized in naming places that are important today.

As an entrepreneur, Sutter saw opportunity all around him and though lacking experience, he had the imagination, drive, and desire to succeed. Sutter became involved in cattle, lumber, trapping, and farming. He relied primarily on the nearby Nisenan and Miwok Indians for cheap labor. One visitor to the fort called him the best "Indian tamer" he had ever seen. A Nisenan later remembered that his people were whipped.

Sutter's enterprise grew into an empire with huge land grants and a country estate that was renowned. Built on credit to finance the operations, he was always negotiating new deals to cover the old ones, staying just ahead of his creditors.

The discovery of gold and the uncontrolled influx of thousands of people into California in 1849 turned his empire upside down. Financially overextended, with many of his staff deserting him for the gold mines, Sutter ultimately lost most of his holdings after a commission was set up to review the validity of the Mexican land grants. With land titles disputed in the course of litigation filed by squatters' associations, the newcomers won the right in U.S. courts to settle in the unmanaged open land.

Land around the Buttes became available for homesteading. Thompson and West's *History of Sutter County* records that in 1849 Edward Thurman settled near the future site of Sutter city. Doc Williams moved in on the east side, and Cullen Lee and Dr. Lee built in Peace Valley by 1850. On the north side, the Evans, Floyd, and Ingraham families settled; while on the west side, Cummins and Lambert built their places by 1851. Within 10 years, many of the families whose descendents still live around the Buttes were a part of the community.

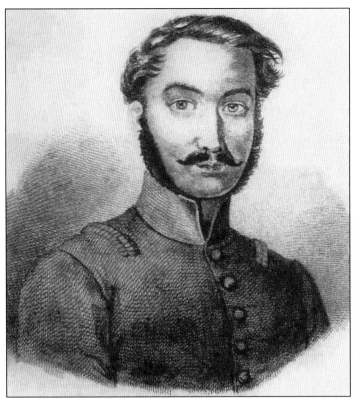

Upon arrival in California by ship in July 1839, John Sutter attended a large social gathering in Monterey. Charming and multilingual, he circulated among prominent politicians and merchants, and he secured financial backing—some authority to act on behalf of Governor Alvarado in California's interior wilderness—and permission to establish a settlement. (California History Room, California State Library, Sacramento.)

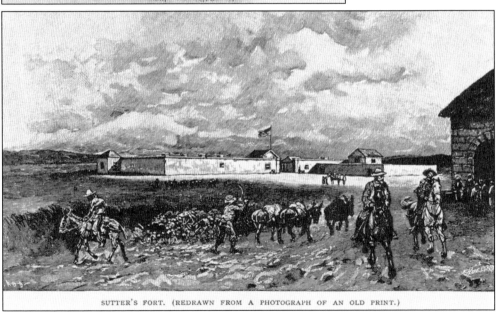

SUTTER'S FORT. (REDRAWN FROM A PHOTOGRAPH OF AN OLD PRINT.)

John Sutter selected a rise east of the confluence of the American and Sacramento rivers for the settlement. Work began to construct wooden shelters thatched with tule reeds. It took four years to build a fort as pictured above. Local Native Americans were enlisted as laborers, first induced with sugar, then clothing, and later homemade metal token money. Firearms were employed to enforce Sutter's authority when his control was tested. (*The Century Magazine*, 1890.)

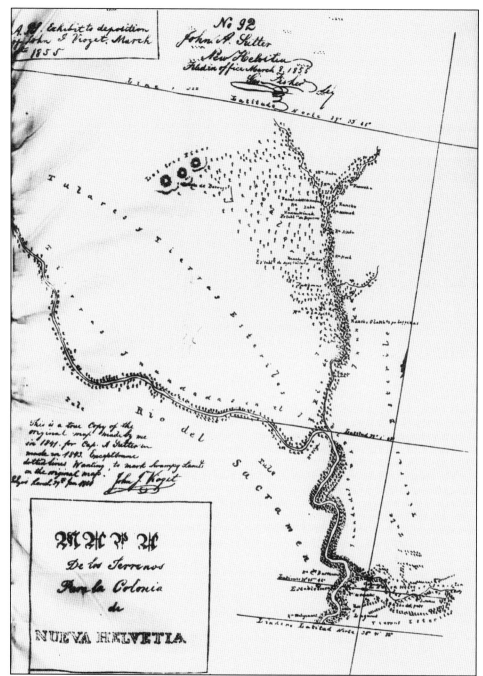

After acquiring Mexican citizenship, Sutter petitioned Governor Alvarado in 1841 for a land grant with a map drawn by his surveyor Jean Jacques Vioget. This copy was redrawn or traced from the original. The first was 11 square leagues in 1841 and a second one of 22 square leagues in 1844. His grants included the Buttes by specific reference, "Bounded on the north by los tres picos; on the east by the border of the Rio de las Plumas; on the south by parallel of 38 degrees, 49 minutes, 32 seconds of north latitude; and on the west by Rio Sacramento." A square league is 4,439 acres. (CMMSC.)

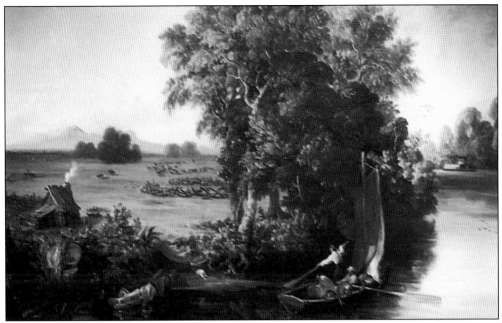

The Butte Mountains loom in the background of this William Smith Jewett 1851 oil painting of the Hock Farm made for Sutter. Jewett was regarded as the "portrait painter to the elite." Inspired by Sutter's descriptions, it portrays an idealistic scene of wilderness life. The farm was on the west side of the Feather River about 5 miles below Yuba City. (California History Room, California State Library, Sacramento.)

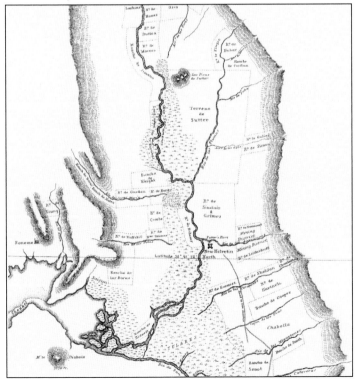

John Bidwell drew the "Mapa del Valle del Sacramento" in 1844 for Mexican governor Micheltorena to illustrate the Sacramento Valley land grants. The distinctive outline represents the edge of the foothills. The broad shaded expanses of "tulares" are swamps. The dotted lines around "terrano de Sutter" delineate Sutter's land grant. "Los Picos de Sutter" is probably the first reference to Sutter's Buttes. (Ron Ross, from *The Blue Oak* by Dorothy Jenkins Ross.)

John Bidwell arrived in California with the first overland wagon train in 1841. He found employment with Sutter and coordinated many management and entrepreneurial projects. In spite of his numerous trips up and down the Sacramento Valley, and an assortment of his descriptive and articulate historical reminiscences, historians find few references to the Buttes. (*The Century Magazine*, 1890.)

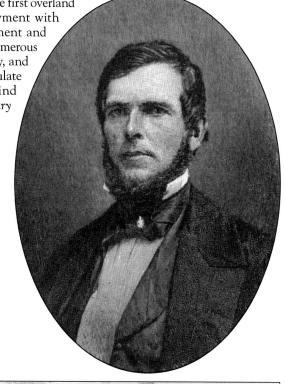

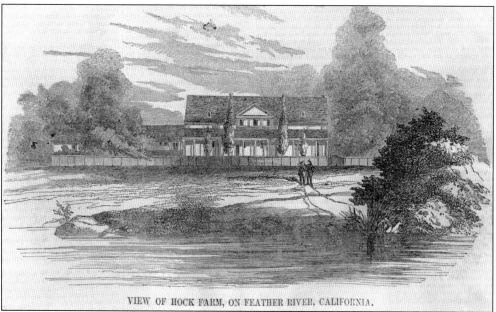

VIEW OF HOCK FARM, ON FEATHER RIVER, CALIFORNIA.

Under Bidwell's supervision, the estate at Hock Farm, a large two-story edifice featuring a portico with a Greek Revival motif, began to take shape. Several acres were fenced off for gardening. Ornamental flowers, orchard trees, and grapes flourished. A staff of 28 maintained the place, and local Native Americans worked the field crops. It became a showplace to feature agricultural productivity, promote land sales, and to finance Sutter's enterprises. (CMMSC.)

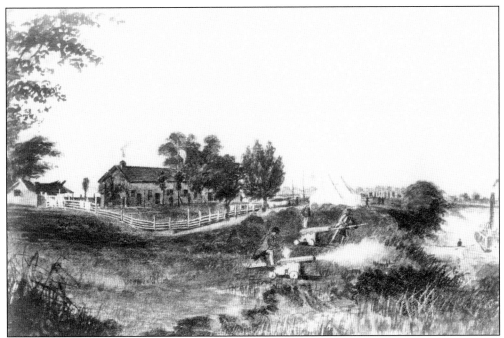

The Hock Farm became a destination to write about. In 1850, the *Sacramento Transcript* published a detailed travelogue of a steamer trip up the river to a grand party hosted by Captain Sutter. A hundred prominent ladies and gentlemen rode the *Governor Dana* steamship—with flags flying and bands playing—up to Sutter's where upon he saluted their arrival with blasts from his cannons. (CMMSC.)

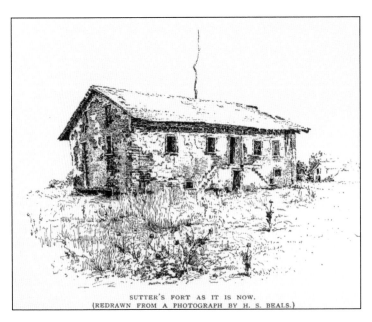

SUTTER'S FORT AS IT IS NOW.
(REDRAWN FROM A PHOTOGRAPH BY H. S. BEALS.)

With the arrival of Sutter's family and his move to the Hock farm, the fort was no longer his base of operations. By the mid-1850s, as heavy winter rains and the departure of Sutter's staff for the gold fields took its toll, the walls and structures were beginning to crumble, a precursor to the future outcome of his empire. (*The Century Magazine,* 1890.)

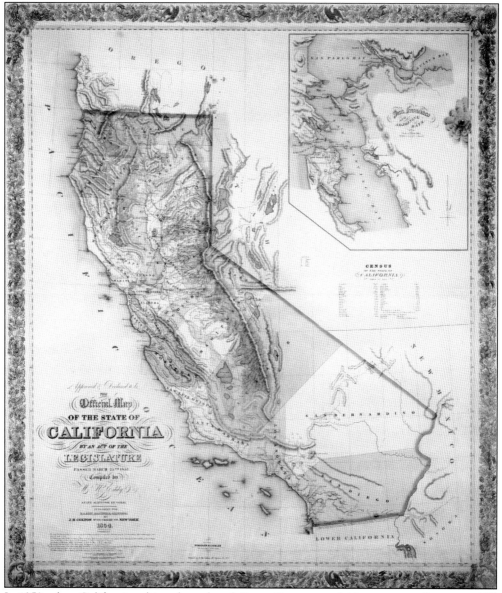

In 1850, when California achieved statehood, Sutter County was laid out as one of its original 27 counties. Its name, drawn from the John Sutter land grant, included much of the land holdings Sutter received from Mexico. Boundaries between Butte and Placer counties were shifted several times before being laid out as we know them today. (California History Room, California State Library, Sacramento.)

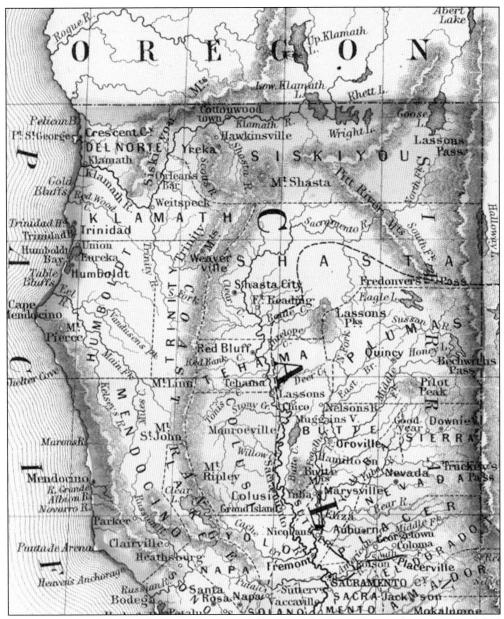

Regarding its northern border, in 1852 statutes delineating the Sutter County lines were modified to include the Buttes in Butte County as follows: "thence in a southeasterly direction to a point at the base of the Buttes, due west of the south point of the same; thence in a northeasterly direction to a point in the middle of the Feather River, opposite the mouth of Honcut Creek." In 1854, it was changed back to a straight line above the Sutter Buttes. (California History Room, California State Library, Sacramento.)

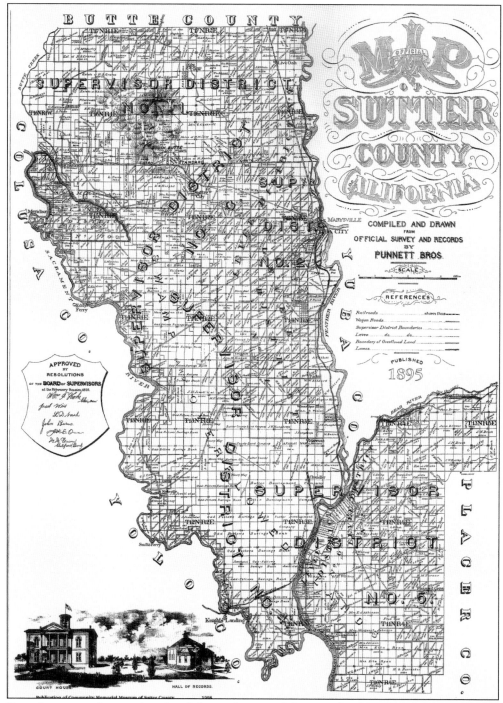

Forty-five years after statehood and the settlement of the open lands in Sutter County, we see the parcel divisions and property lines with larger holdings identified by family name. Each small square is a 160-acre parcel—four of them make a square mile. Most of the wagon roads shown here are now the country roads that we still use today. This map has been reprinted in a legible full-size format and can be purchased at the local museum. (CMMSC.)

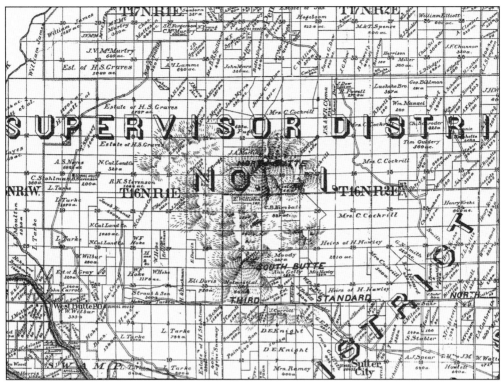

Enlarging the map enables one to inspect the property ownership around the Buttes in the late 1800s. Note the names on the map and refer back to this page as you peruse the photographs in the rest of our collection. The descendents of many of these families still own property in and around the Buttes. The lineage of some is not evident when the daughters marry and assume the name of their husband. On the south side, for example, Donna McMasters is a descendent of the Brockman family and on the north side the Shaeffers have descended from the Myers. (CMMSC.)

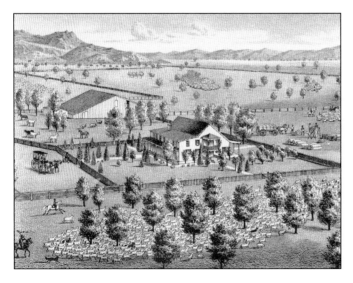

Dr. William McMurtry acquired a 160-acre homestead on the north side of the Buttes in 1851, but other endeavors postponed his farming involvement for three years. By 1875, the family owned 2,744 acres. Landowners were offered a place in the *History of Sutter County* for a price to underwrite the publication expense. Note the details of the sheep operation. (Thompson and West's *History of Sutter County, California.*)

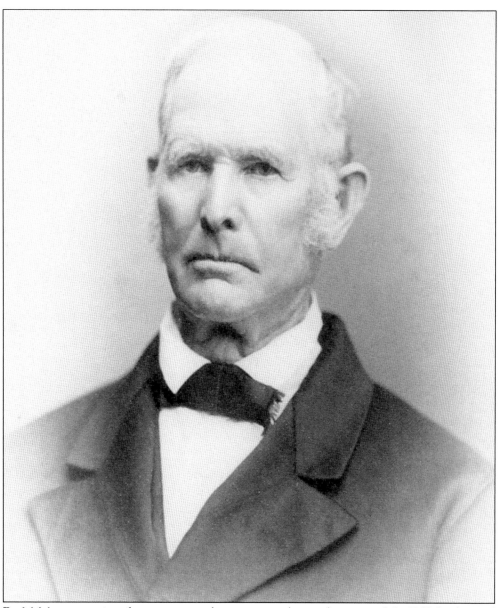

Dr. McMurtry continued to practice medicine even as the ranch prospered. In 1868, he donated land for the local school. His wife, Sarah, died, and he later married her sister, Cynthia. They moved to Oakland where he died in 1892. He is buried in the North Butte Cemetery where the family erected a tall spire to honor his passing. Their ranching business was passed down through the family. (Brian McMurtry.)

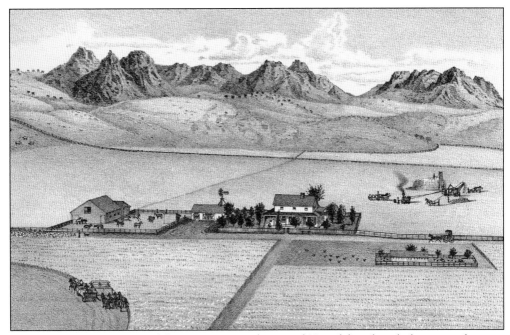

Henry S. Graves came to California in 1849 at the age of 19 and found work driving pack teams up to the gold mines. He acquired a squatter's title to land on the northwest edge of the Buttes and began building there in 1852. By 1888 the family had accumulated 4,000 acres and engaged in raising sheep and farming wheat and barley. (Thompson and West's *History of Sutter County, California*.)

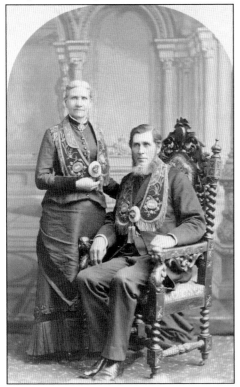

In 1862, Graves married Mary Terstegge Darple, a young widow, and began building a fine home. They raised six children. Affiliation with a social (or service) organization or fraternal order was a measure of one's standing in the community at that time, and the couple is pictured here in such finery. Graves was a member of the Pioneer Society, North Butte Grange, and the Good Templars. (CMMSC.)

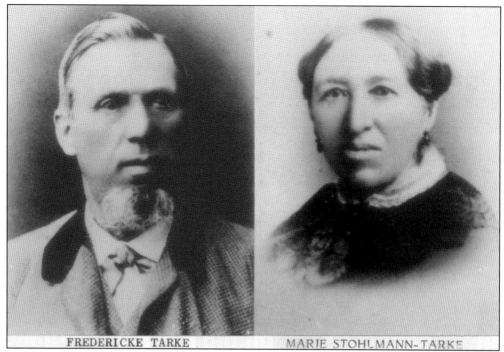

FREDERICKE TARKE   MARIE STOHLMANN-TARKE

Frederick Tarke came to California in 1850 on a wagon train with companion Frederick Hoke. They worked the mines for several seasons, returned to Iowa where each married and came back to the Golden State in 1856. They jointly acquired title to 160 acres on the southwest flank of the Buttes. The ranch prospered and Tarke, along with his bride Marie, raised three children, Annie, Emma, and Louis. (CMMSC.)

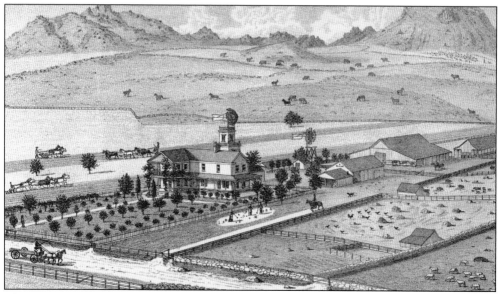

The Tarke-Hoke partnership flourished, and as each family acquired surrounding lands, they decided to separate their operations. The Tarke home pictured here was substantially remodeled in 1885 by son Louis sometime after he took over running the ranch. The stately home is still occupied by the Tarke family today. (Thompson and West's *History of Sutter County, California*.)

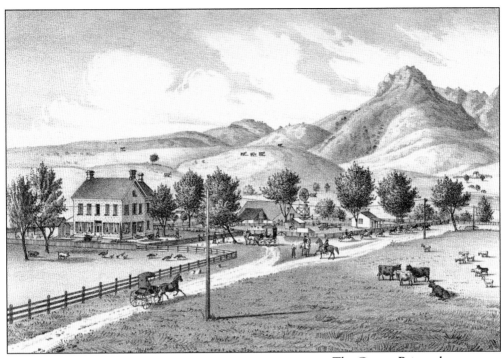

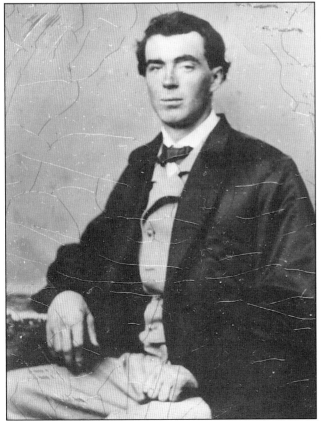

The George Brittan house was a seven-year project completed in 1869. Most remarkable about this home is the stone walls that were quarried down the road in the Buttes. A full 18 inches thick, each stone was laboriously cut by drilling holes into the rock, then driving in wooden stakes that were moistened until they swelled, splitting the stones into rectangular blocks. (Thompson and West's *History of Sutter County, California*.)

Aaron Pugh was a forty-niner who acquired property in the North Butte area in 1854. In the summers he packed supplies to the mines; in the winters he farmed in the Buttes. He married three times and lost each wife to illness. Next to a spring against the mountain, he built a home with broad, covered porches and a hand pump for water right on the porch. (Mary Spilman Crane.)

Five

BUTTES FAMILIES

Cemetery tombstones, old maps, and county records contain the names of early Sutter Buttes settlers and pioneers. Historical society bulletins detail many of these family histories. Their stories, like John Sutter's, convey the determination, perseverance, and enterprise that fueled America's westward expansion across thousands of miles of wilderness, or rough seas, through months of toil and hardship, to finally settle in the shadow of the Sutter Buttes.

These experiences are collected by the descendents of those families in footlockers or in shoe boxes tucked away on closet shelves or the bottom of bookcases. They are in the form of handwritten journals, penciled notes, framed portraits, old photographs in black-paged albums, envelopes full of negatives, or creased and tattered old documents. They are a source of pride and inspiration to those families who saved these mementoes of their forefathers' accomplishments. Some families have detailed notes with names and dates; some know only which one is grandpa and grandma. But all of them have fond memories of growing up and living in the country around the mountain.

A compilation of these archives creates a mosaic blending of diversity that forms a larger story, revealing a deep connection to the landscape. Busy lives, and even the mountain itself, separate these families physically by miles, but a shared heritage links and connects them emotionally. Most of their households today display a panoramic photograph or painting of the familiar silhouette of the Sutter Buttes on the wall. The photographs and memorabilia in this chapter will resonate with those who lived this country life, whether it was near the Buttes or far away.

Unfortunately, time and space constraints limit the inclusion of everyone's photographs into a small project such as this. The scenes selected here are reminiscent of the experiences of many residents. It is hoped that the fondness and familiarity of the names and places pictured here will engender people to dust off their personal archives and show them to family and friends or consider donating them to local museums and historical societies where they will be preserved and added to Buttes' local heritage.

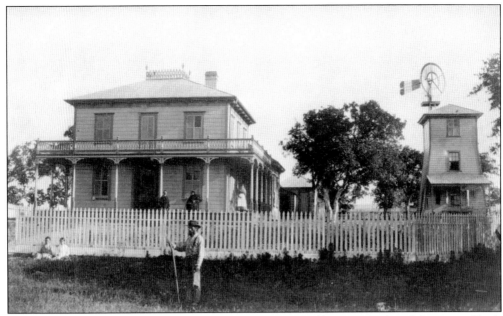

In 1866, William Powell acquired 198 acres on a patent signed by Pres. Andrew Johnson and built near the intersection of Pennington and Powell Roads, northeast of the Buttes. His son, Richard, who is pictured here around 1885, built this home shortly before the photograph was taken. The home burned in 1929 with a great loss of old pictures, mementos, and journals. (Rick Powell.)

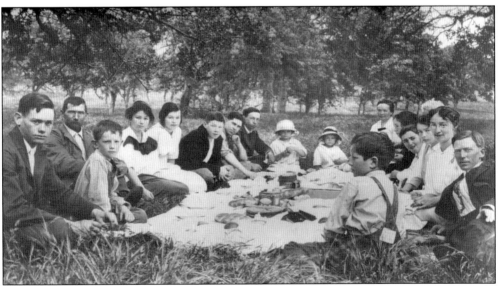

In this 1913 photograph, the Powell family spread out a blanket and gathered in close. One of the family members took the time to label everyone by name on the back of the photograph. The dark-haired mother, Annie, is seated at the very back of the photograph. The Powells still celebrate an annual springtime family reunion in Dow Grove. (Rick Powell.)

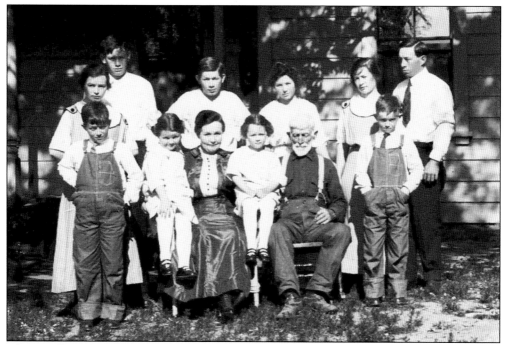

The Powells sat for a family portrait alongside the house around 1900. Ten of their eleven children are pictured. The twins, Agnes and Alice, are sitting on the armrest of their mother's chair. Agnes was prominently situated in the picnic photograph on the left side, towards the back. (Brian McMurtry.)

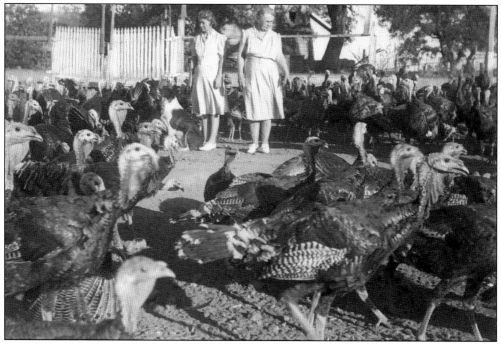

This undated photograph of Anne Powell and her turkeys was probably taken in the 1930s. Her hair is graying, and the kids have all grown up. (Rick Powell.)

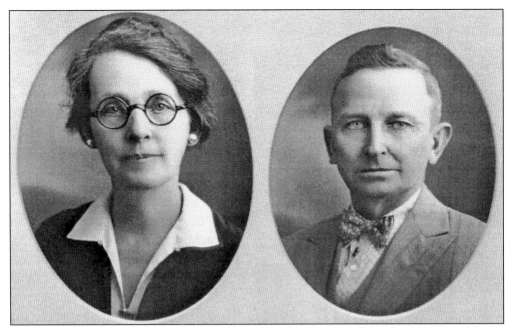

The McPherrin family first settled around the Buttes in 1854. John Jacob McPherrin, pictured above, married Annastacia Gibson in 1895. They invested in the sheep business in 1916, buying 100 sheep at a dollar each, and in 1919 partnered with their son Elwood to acquire the ranch off East Butte Road where the family still lives today. (*The Long Way to Make a Million*, by Calvert McPherrin.)

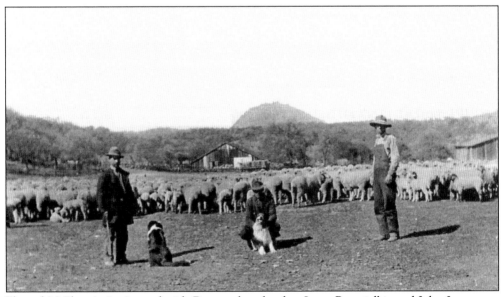

Elwood McPherrin is pictured with Basque sheepherders Leon Berrojalbiz and John Laurnaga. Elwood's son, Calvert, later wrote, "The ranch was pretty much an open range operation. Sheep and lambs were kept in brush corrals at night." (Calvert McPherrin.)

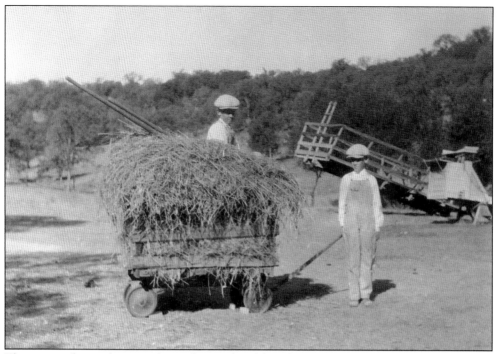

There were always chores to do on the ranch. Although a year apart, Calvert and his brother, Fayne, started school together. By the seventh grade they were driving themselves to school because their mother had to stay home with a new baby boy. (Calvert McPherrin.)

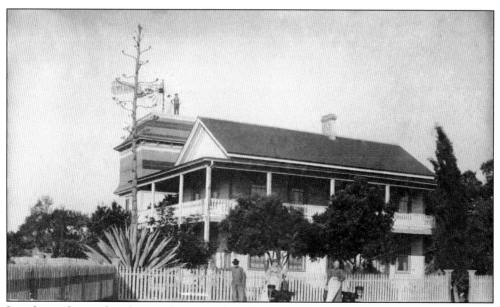

Just down the road is the stately Howard residence. Historians record that it was once the Philadelphia House hotel in Marysville. Dr. E. J. Howard completed renovations in 1866. The tank house that was built in the 1880s and the agave century plant help to estimate the date of this photograph to be before 1900. (CMMSC.)

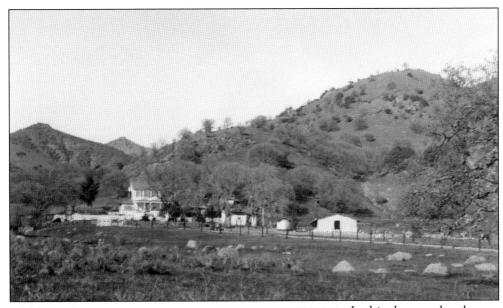

In this photograph, taken around 1948, the old Moore Place is pictured off Pass Road, tucked back in a shady canyon. In 1861, it was built upon 8-inch timbers set on a flat rock foundation. T. J. Moore bought it from the Getty family in 1900. Grandson Lance Cull said they did not receive electricity until 1937. (Lance Cull.)

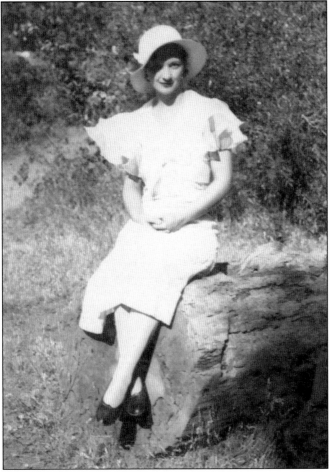

Esther Eileen Moore, shown in this c. 1926 photograph, was born in 1906. Her son Lance Cull wrote, "Mom told me that the lantern on the back porch never stopped swinging for 60 days after those San Francisco earthquakes." Esther married Howard Cull. Lance and his sister Autumn were raised in that ranch house. (Lance Cull.)

70

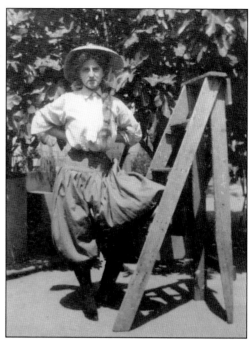

Eleta Hill attended West Butte school as a youngster and returned later to live at her parents' home in West Butte and teach in the area. Her hat, hair, skirt, boots, and demeanor express a spirited personality. (Donna McMasters.)

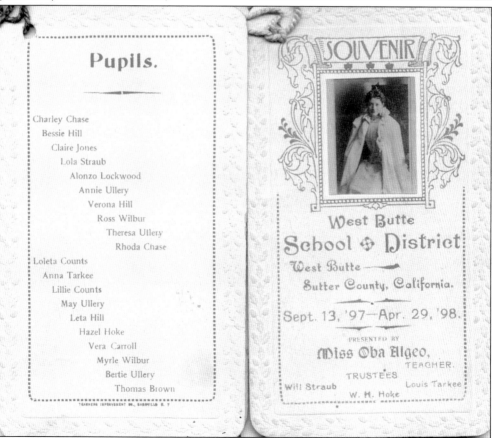

Pupils.

Charley Chase
Bessie Hill
Claire Jones
Lola Straub
Alonzo Lockwood
Annie Ullery
Verona Hill
Ross Wilbur
Theresa Ullery
Rhoda Chase
Loleta Counts
Anna Tarkee
Lillie Counts
May Ullery
Leta Hill
Hazel Hoke
Vera Carroll
Myrle Wilbur
Bertie Ullery
Thomas Brown

SOUVENIR

West Butte
School ☩ District
West Butte——
Sutter County, California.

Sept. 13, '97—Apr. 29, '98.

PRESENTED BY
Miss Oba Algeo,
TEACHER.
TRUSTEES
Will Straub   Louis Tarkee
W. H. Hoke

California Sketches

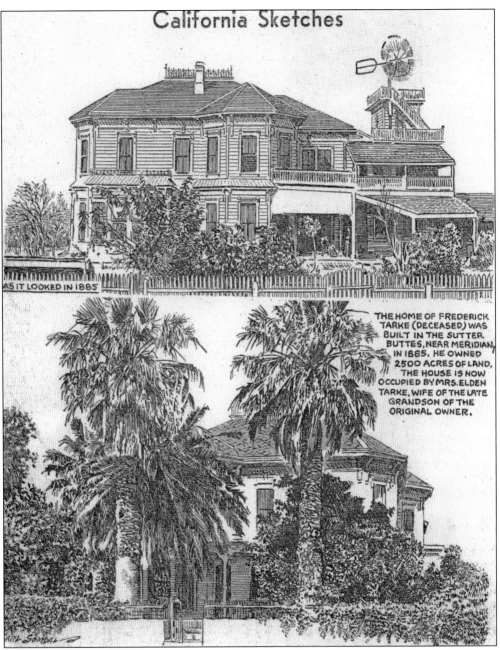

AS IT LOOKED IN 1885

THE HOME OF FREDERICK TARKE (DECEASED) WAS BUILT IN THE SUTTER BUTTES, NEAR MERIDIAN, IN 1885. HE OWNED 2500 ACRES OF LAND. THE HOUSE IS NOW OCCUPIED BY MRS. ELDEN TARKE, WIFE OF THE LATE GRANDSON OF THE ORIGINAL OWNER.

Community appreciation of a family legacy that comes from maintaining a historic old house can be felt by the publicity and museum sponsored drive-by tours that the Tarke house continues to receive. A local historian tells a story about a wooded grove to the west of the home that is likewise preserved and captured on a painting that is 100 years old. (CMMSC.)

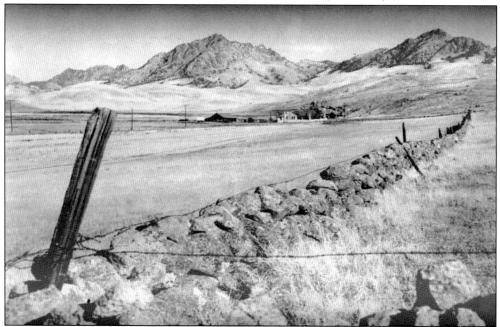

The old Wilbur home is gone. Some of the family is buried in the nearby Noyesburg Cemetery. The home, pictured here at the back of the lane, now belongs to the Steidlmayer family. A historic document that came with the property was this land grant signed by the president of the United States, Ulysses S. Grant, conferring ownership to Willis W. Wilbur on March 15, 1869. Numerous Buttes families have inherited these presidential grants. (Marty Steidlmayer.)

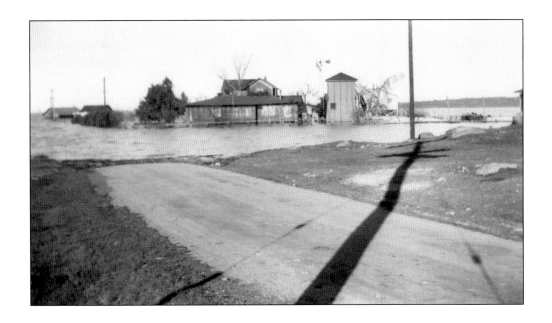

The Sacramento Outing Club on West Butte Road provides one with an interesting perspective of the Sutter Buttes landscape. Leroy Pennington spent a lifetime out there and shares these photographs. Heavy winter rains can fill up the Butte sink lowlands. Then it overflows onto the roadway, closing off the backside of the mountain to vehicular traffic. Rare winter snows prompted everyone to retrieve their cameras. It seldom snows this deep in the Sacramento Valley. These buildings burned down in 1952. The images were taken around 1941 and 1936, respectively. (Leroy Pennington.)

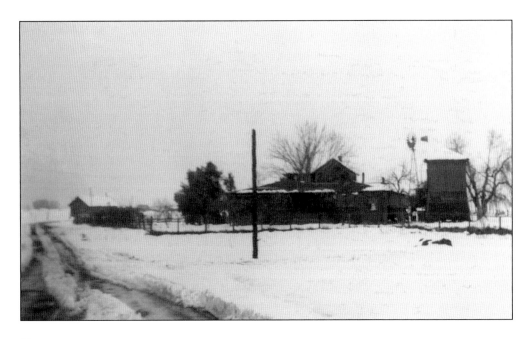

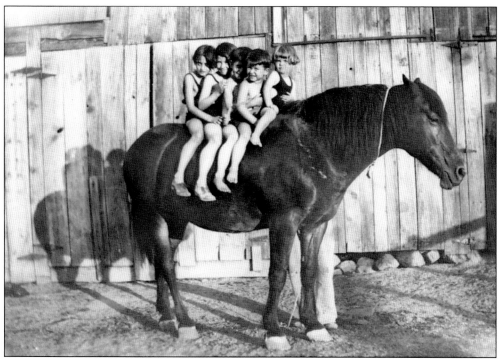

Growing up in a duck club is just like everywhere else, right? In this photograph, taken around 1934, are, from left to right, Delia, Naomi, Leroy, Lloyd, and Wini Pennington all seated on "Johnie." Father Fred Pennington is behind the horse, holding up the little ones. (Leroy Pennington.)

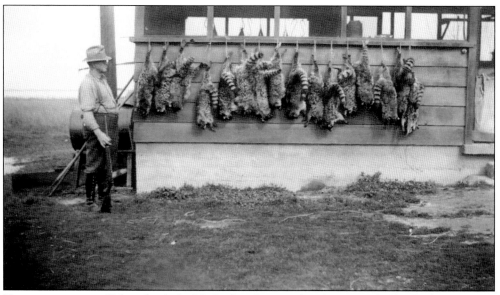

Hunting was a way of life at the duck club. In this photograph, taken around 1930, Fred Pennington inspects his catch of raccoons, which were considered a nuisance and a threat to nesting waterfowl. Leroy remembers that the 'coons were skinned and sold. (Leroy Pennington.)

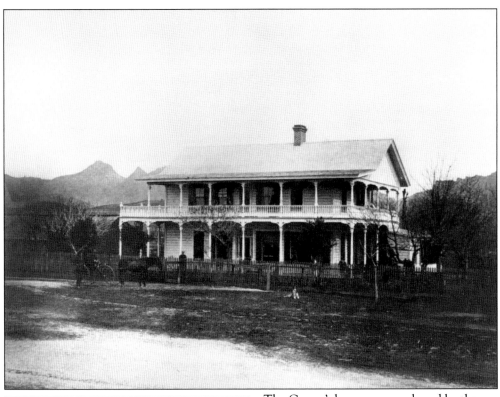

The Graves's home was purchased by the Thomas Brady family after Mrs. Graves passed in 1917. This is the same home pictured in the lithograph on page 62. The most significant change to it was the addition of the covered porch on the second floor. Descendents of the Bradys still own land in the Buttes, but this property is now in the Tarke family. (CMMSC.)

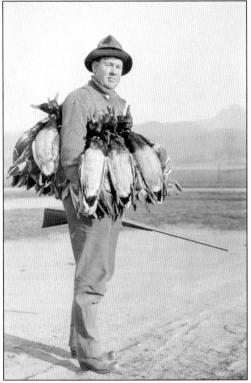

Allen Noyes, a forty-niner, was one of the earliest settlers on the west side of the Buttes. He donated land for the local school and cemetery. Pictured here in this c. 1915 photograph is Noyes's grandson, Charles Noyes, who did not mind walking a mile to hunt in the wetlands of the nearby Butte Sink. (CMMSC.)

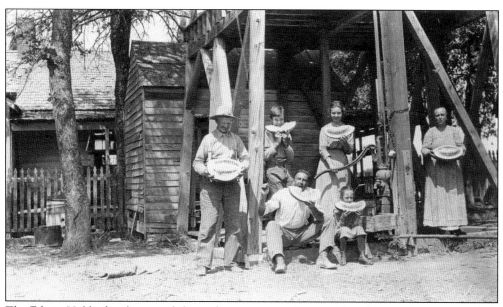

The Edwin Hubbs family treated themselves to watermelon on a hot August afternoon in 1910. Pictured here are, from left to right, (first row) an enthusiastic neighbor and Lena; (second row) Edwin, Harold, Anna, and Mother Alice Clyma Hubbs. (Barbara Dow Kamilos.)

A bicycle is a smoother ride than a horse. "My mother, Anna, and grandma each have a bike, but Grandpa Edwin Hubbs' cycle looks heavy enough to be a motorcycle. This house used to be known as the old Spilman Place. The Derees live there now," said Barbara. This photograph was taken around 1915. (Barbara Dow Kamilos.)

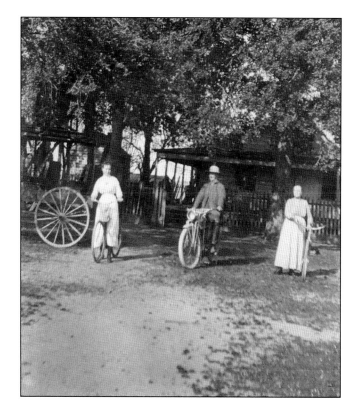

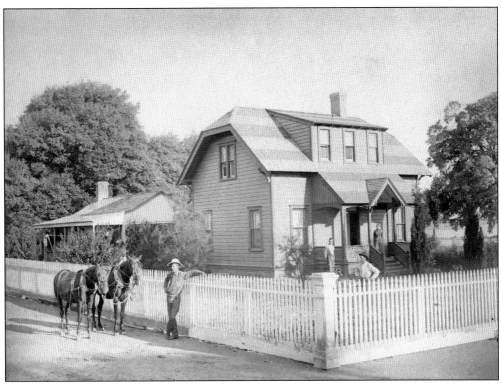

This attractive and compact home, located in a valley of the Buttes, has been in the same family since the 1860s. Old maps identify the parcels owned by J. H. Myers. It is a treat to get both sides of the family together for photographs. In the bottom left image are (first row) Mary Elizabeth Myers Bonslett, Gladys Myers Shaeffer, and George Henry Myers; (second row) John Calvin Myers. In the bottom right image are (first row) Raymond Shaeffer, father of Gary and Tyrone; (second row) John Shaeffer holding Gary and Gladys Myers Shaeffer holding Tyrone; (third row) Malinda Aulman Shaeffer. Ray is in his 90s today. The image of the house was taken around 1880 and the bottom two about 1947. (Tyrone Shaeffer.)

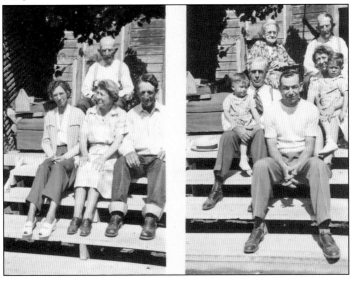

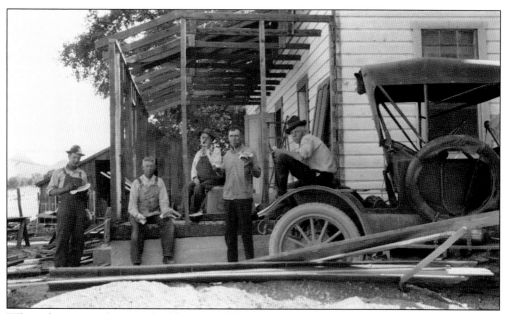

When the crew—that was building an addition to the J. McMurtry home on North Butte—stopped for lunch, around 1915, it was also an opportunity to snap a photograph of the progress. (Brian McMurtry.)

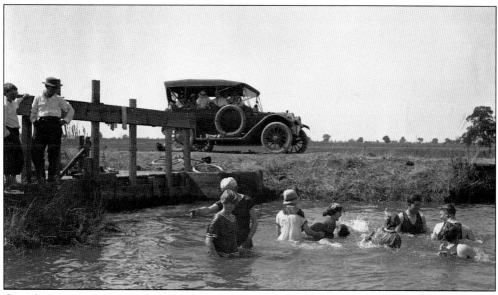

On a hot, summer day, nothing beats swimming. Pennington resident and photographer Billy McMurtry captured this scene around 1915. For residents who lived way out in the country in the early 1900s, the best way to cope with the heat was by cooling off in the irrigation canals and ditches. (Brian McMurtry.)

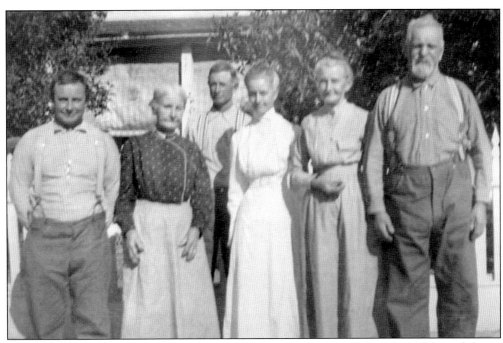

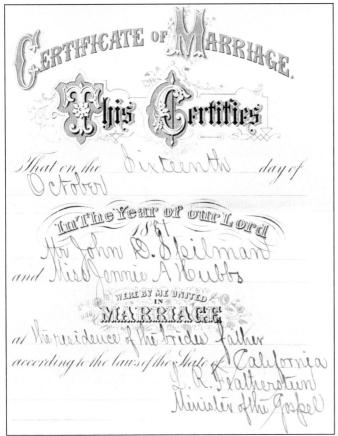

When the Hubbs and the Spilmans got together, they were more than just friends and neighbors, they were family. Pictured here around 1921 are, from left to right, Norman Hubbs, Elizabeth Straid Hubbs, Louis Hubbs, Hannah Hubbs with Jennie Hubbs Spilman, and J. D. Spilman. The Spilmans' marriage certificate dates back to 1881. (Barbara Dow Kamilos.)

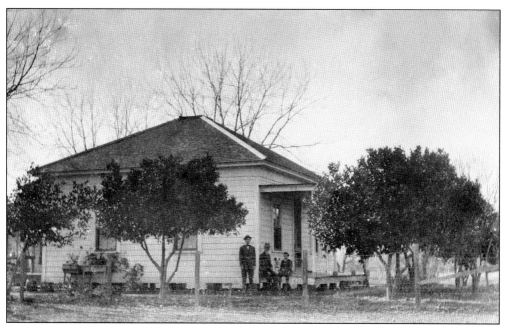

The Spilman cottage is situated in the old town site of Pennington. There are three generations of Spilmans buried in the nearby cemetery. The house has been expanded, and Janet Spilman still maintains a residence in the quaint, old cottage. (Mary Spilman Crane.)

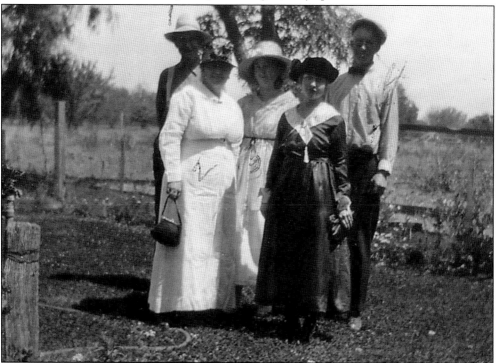

Some of the Ballard family gathered together for this photograph. Father and mother, Lee Ally and Nettie Louella, along with daughter-in-law, Evelyn; daughter, Rosemary; and son, Bert, posed beyond the flower garden in 1918. (Dorothy Rae Redhair Coats.)

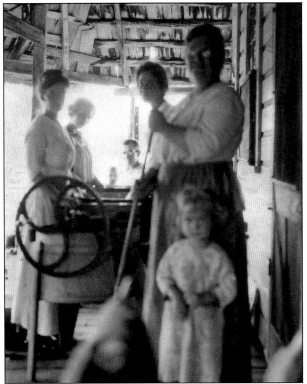

In 1915, wash day for the Lee Ally and Nettie Louella Ballard family on the porch occasionally involved three generations. Grandchild Beth Adams is pictured in the foreground in front of Nettie Louella. Behind Nettie, over the washtubs, are, from left to right, daughters Blanch and Rosemary, and daughter-in-law, Evelyn. Grandson Arthur Adams is at the back next to Lee Ally. (Dorothy Rae Redhair Coats.)

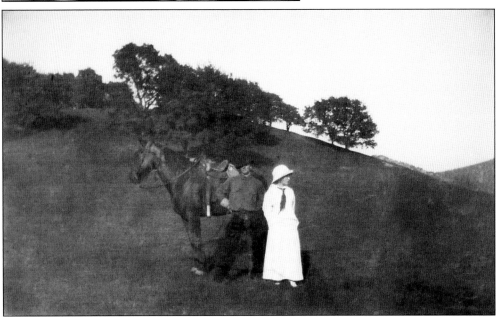

This photograph of Raymond Redhair and Rosemary Ballard from 1915 was one of the many times they were photographed together. She once described him as her "best friend." He gave her a ruby ring when she was 14. Raymond was seven years older than Rosemary, and he had to go off to World War I but returned and married her in 1921. The ring is still in the family. (Dorothy Rae Redhair Coats.)

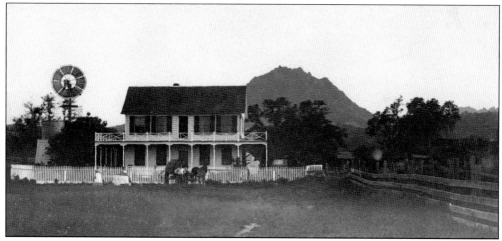

The Thomas and Anne Clyma home was a substantial edifice with all the accoutrements of the day. Just months before this Buttes history project was initiated, the one family member who was researching his family roots passed away. Ron Clyma spent most of his life in Sacramento, but those who remember him know that his heart was in the Buttes, where he is now buried. (Barbara Dow Kamilos.)

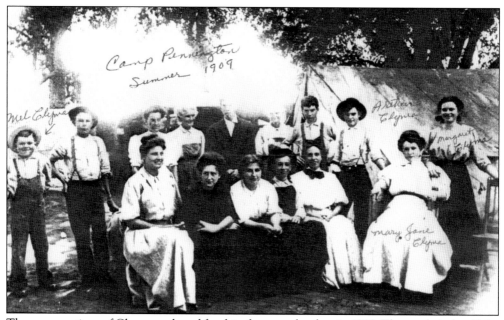

Three generations of Clymas gathered for this photograph taken in 1909. The puzzle is that if the Clymas had such a fine house in the North Butte area, why is this labeled "Camp Pennington?" Is the camp overflow attendance from a family reunion? (Barbara Clyma Nicholaus.)

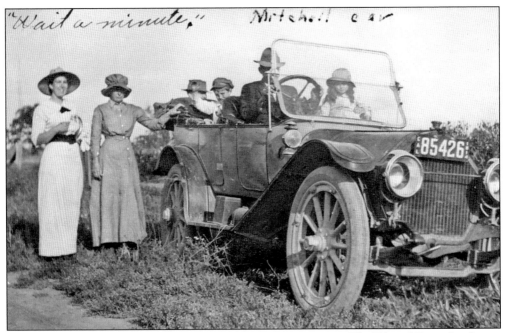

"Wait a minute," Mitchell car

The Edward Dean family had a small ranch house in the Buttes, but they drove in, as they did not live there year-round. Members of the Dean family are pictured in their Mitchell car. The car was state-of-the-art for its time, and owning one in 1914 was a source of pride. (Margit Sands.)

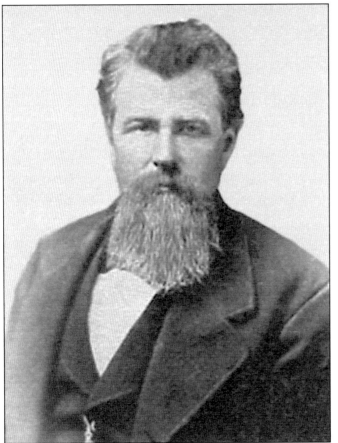

Capt. Thomas Dean is remembered in Sutter County history as the leader of the Sutter County Home Guard, a 22-man squad that raised an 80-foot flagpole atop South Butte on July 4, 1861, in support of the Union army during the Civil War. The Edward Dean family knew him as Uncle Thomas. (Margit Sands.)

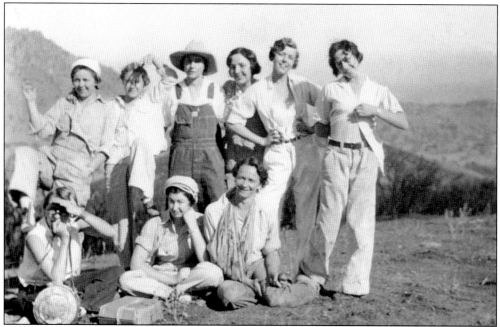

High school friends in the Buttes, away from stern parental eyes, had fun flirting for the photographer in 1931. Shirley Dean, in the bibs and straw hat, was good friends with Nadean Lydecker to her right and Lucinda Messick to her left. Teacher Dot Edgar, with her arm in a sling, was a mentor to Shirley, 98 years old at the time of this book's publication in early 2010. (Margit Sands.)

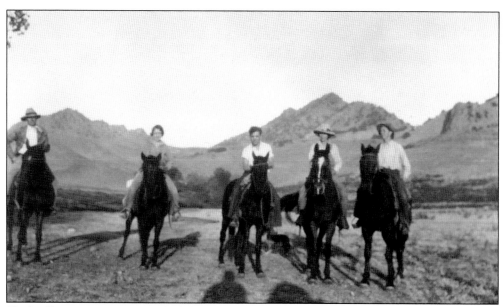

Shirley Dean is seen again in the bibs and straw hat in November 1930. While her photo album names the people in this picture, horse-lovers will connect with this photograph because it names the mounts as well. Pictured here, the horses are, from left to right, Kid, Brown Beauty, Mike, Whiz Bang (Shirley's horse), and Happy. (Margit Sands.)

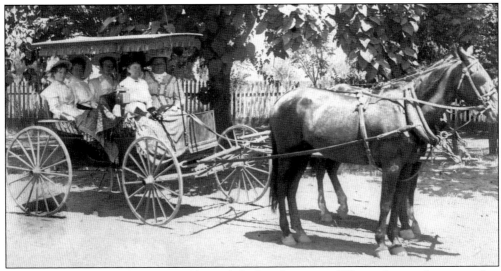

This photograph turned up in two files with little information. What is known for sure is that the pretty Pennington ladies are dressed for a trip, around 1908. (CMMSC.)

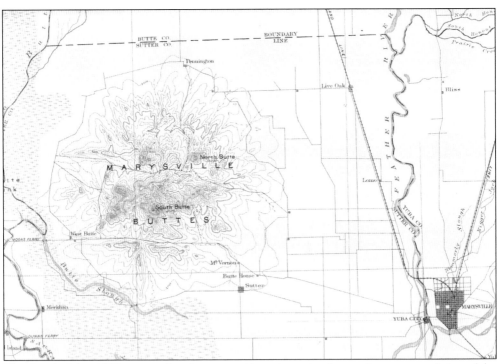

The detail of this 1895 topographical map provides orientation for touring towns and sites of the Buttes around the beginning of the 20th century. The roadways were mostly dirt wagon trails. Pass Road—through the lower portion of the mountain range—was the more direct route between Colusa and Marysville. Noting the comparative sizes of the towns, it is clear why the range was called Marysville Buttes. (YCLCR.)

Six

TOWNS AROUND
THE BUTTES

Every town site started with one settler and an enterprise. Most seem to be a day's walk or ride away from the next town. Some old sites flourished for a while and then withered like a plant without water. Those that grew were along a thoroughfare, at an intersection, a river, or perhaps near valuable resources. The histories of both are evident around the Buttes once we examine old maps, publications, and stories.

Southwest of the Buttes, against the Sacramento River, Meridian was settled in 1852. John Fouts established a ferry and a small store there by 1860, and four years later a town was laid out and lots were being sold. The name of Meridian was selected due to its alignment with the Mount Diablo Meridian.

A little cabin was built near the southeastern edge of the Buttes in 1854. Isaac Tyndall built on to it in the spring of 1856, and he opened the Butte House and hosted a July Fourth celebration, dinner, dance, and a wedding. By 1871, it was established as the South Butte Post Office, receiving daily mail delivered by the Marysville and Colusa Stage. In 1887, entrepreneur Peter Gardemeyer orchestrated a grandiose scheme to develop the area into a metropolis called Sutter City.

In 1868, the first settler, in the area that became known as Live Oak, was A. M. McGrew. Ten years later there were a store, two blacksmith shops, 25 dwellings, a school, a church, a post office, a Wells Fargo express office, a train station, and a saloon.

Just west of the Buttes there were several homes clustered, so a school was started in 1860. A store was built in 1867, which soon served as the post office, making its name West Butte official. Four miles up the road, Noyesburg came into being when Allen Noyes opened a blacksmith shop and donated land for a school and cemetery. On the north side of the Buttes, the town of Pennington was laid out in 1880.

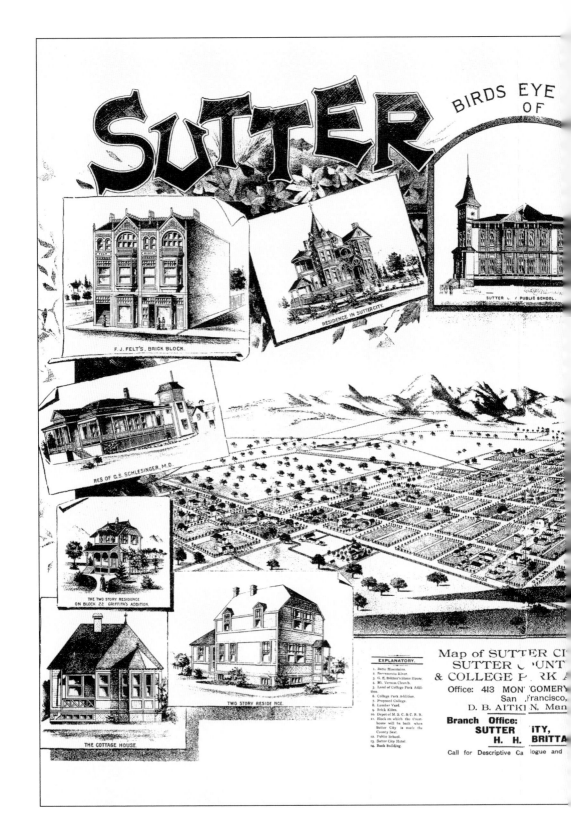

SUTTER

BIRDS EYE
OF

F. J. FELT'S, BRICK BLOCK.

RESIDENCE IN SUTTER CITY.

SUTTER CITY PUBLIC SCHOOL.

RES OF G.S. SCHLESINGER, M.D.

THE TWO STORY RESIDENCE
ON BLOCK 22 GRIFFITH'S ADDITION.

TWO STORY RESIDENCE.

THE COTTAGE HOUSE.

EXPLANATORY.

1. Butte Mountains.
2. Sacramento River.
3. G. E. Brittan's Stone House.
4. Mt. Vernon Church.
5. Land of College Park Addition.
6. College Park Addition.
7. Proposed College.
8. Lumber Yard.
9. Brick Kilns.
10. Depot of M. S. C. & C. R.R.
11. Block on which the Court-house will be built when Sutter City is made the County Seat.
12. Public School.
13. Sutter City Hotel.
14. Bank Building.

Map of SUTTER CITY
SUTTER COUNTY
& COLLEGE PARK A

Office: 413 MONTGOMERY
San Francisco,
D. B. AITKEN, Man

Branch Office:
SUTTER CITY,
H. H. BRITTA

Call for Descriptive Catalogue and

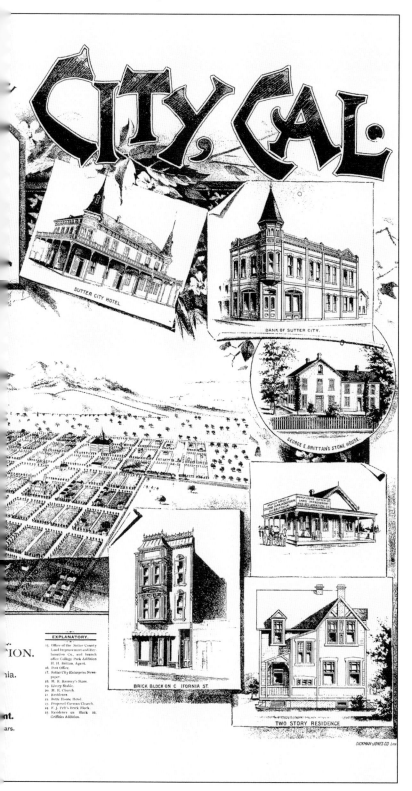

Peter D. Gardemeyer reportedly arrived in the Buttes area in 1884 selling sewing machines and patented farm gates. He must have been a gregarious and persuasive individual, as he soon married a "widow of considerable means," according to one local historian. He then connected with some business partners in San Francisco and purchased 640 acres to develop a city that he promised would become the county seat. He collaborated to form the Sutter County Land Improvement and Reclamation Company in 1888. One thousand shares of stock were issued for $100 each. Homesites were sold for $200 and up. The poster pictured at left promotes the enterprise, complete with the additional College Park tract and the proposed rail line that was planned to pass through the area. He also planned a resort hotel in the Buttes, but the building boom faltered, and he ended up in debt, leaving town by 1891. (CMMSC.)

89

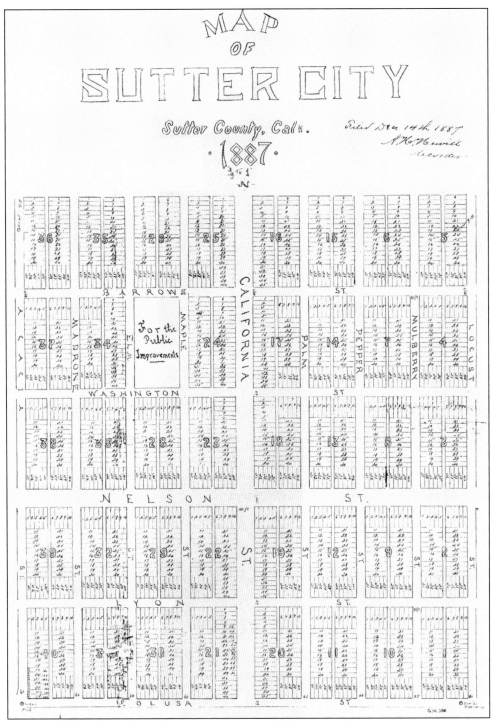

The Sutter City plat plan was filed December 14, 1887. The plan specified California and Nelson Streets as 100-foot-wide thoroughfares and 39 blocks with 50 lots, 25 feet by 125 feet. One block was set aside for "public improvements." Compare this plan to the poster. (Sutter County Public Records, Ron Smith.)

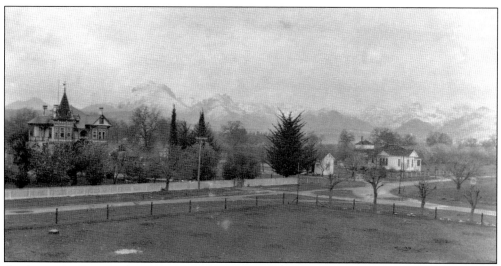

Gardemeyer constructed a mansion on the west end of Nelson Street for his new wife, the former Mary Charlotte Erke, and her children. The novelty of a snowfall on the Buttes probably prompted this photograph. Several years after Gardemeyer left town, a disgruntled investor who had lost his savings shot and killed Mary Charlotte Gardemeyer. (CMMSC.)

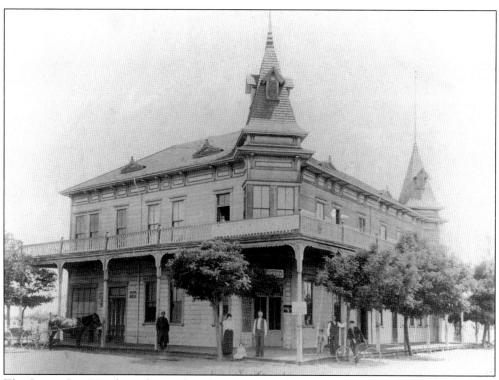

The Sutter City Hotel was featured in the promotional poster. On the back of the photograph, Verna McLean, whose father operated a store there, wrote, "I had a choice of 15 rooms upstairs . . . to hide." The site is now the location of the Sutter Post Office. (CMMSC.)

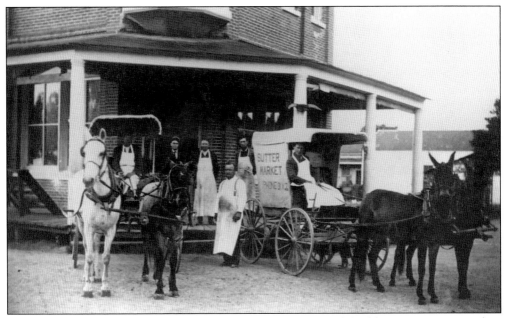

Built to be a bank as part of Gardemeyer's promotion, this brick building was a meat market, as pictured here; a library; and a meeting hall for the Native Daughters' organization. Three of the men were named on the back of this photograph: Bert Paxton in the dark suit, Bill Hill on the ground, and Norman Haynes behind him. The building stands deserted now at the same intersection. (CMMSC.)

An 1897 newspaper ad published in the *Sutter County Farmer* for the McLean and Hardman's Store located in the hotel building advertises sale prices of 5¢, 10¢, 25¢, and 50¢ for everything but the coffee. (Donna McMasters.)

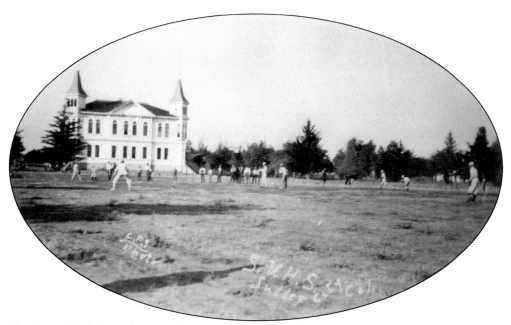

The Sutter High School was on the upper floor of the schoolhouse. The schoolhouse was one of the first structures built as a part of Sutter City. Their baseball games took place on the broad, flat field adjoining the school grounds. As pictured in 1900, the players have uniforms, but the site lacks the refinements of a baseball diamond that is taken for granted today. (CMMSC.)

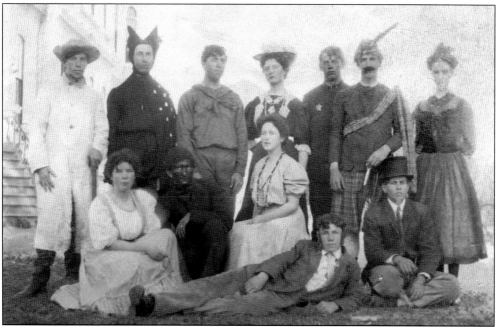

Posing in front of the SUHS, a dozen students are costumed for an unidentified dramatic production. Many of these family names are still in the community today. Pictured here are, from left to right, (first row) Ruth Keran, Fred Havens, Lou Huff, Elwin Paxton, and Herman Lemenager, the villain; (second row) David Addington, Alvin Weis, Gus Kirk, Inez Mehl Close, Lee Morehead, Parker Reische, and Bessie King. (CMMSC.)

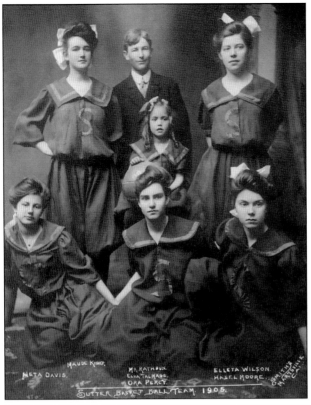

This Sutter High School girls' basketball team portrait is a keepsake for seven families and a jewel to find for a photograph montage such as this publication. In this 1905 photograph are, from left to right, (first row) Neta Davis, Ora Percy, and Hazel Moore; (second row) Maude King, little Elva Talmadge holding the ball, and Elleta Wilson; (third row) coach Rathbun. (CMMSC.)

Union School was situated west of East Butte Road below Sanders Road. Assumption Lang Coats taught grades first through eighth there. The students are dressed up in this photograph, but only the boy with the lily is identified as Joseph Miner Burns. Just up the road from the school was the site of the Methodist Camp Bethel revival services held annually under a 100-by-100-feet square tent-covered pavilion. (CMMSC)

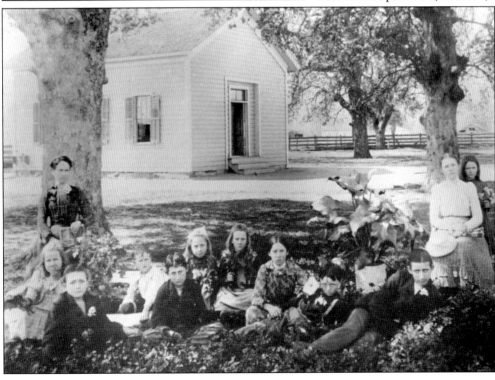

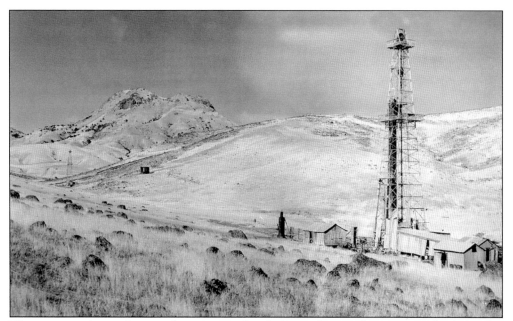

The presence of natural gas was long suspected in the Buttes because fires continued to burn after the plant life was blackened. In 1864, a mine shaft exploded due to the fumes, confirming these theories. After repeated attempts, drilling practices improved, and the first commercial production began in 1933. The first rig went to a depth of 2,727 feet and pumped 3.4 million cubic feet of gas each day. This photograph was taken around 1940. (YCLCR.)

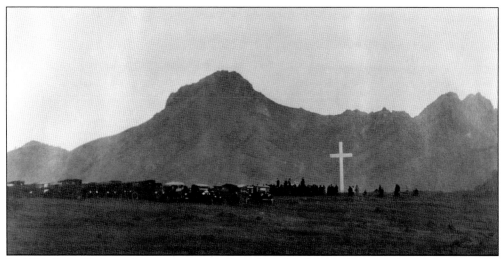

In 1921, E. S. Wadsworth was instrumental in planning the first Easter sunrise services in the Buttes. His grandson, Austin Lemenager, born in 1921, has participated in hosting this tradition as long as he can remember. The Lemenager family hosts this event every year. (CMMSC.)

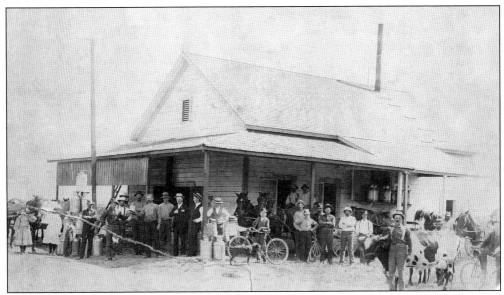

It was quite an occasion when the photographer announced he wanted to take a picture. Everyone nearby came over to the Meridian Creamery to be in this 1900 photograph. A note on the back identifies Al Blackmer as the man just left of center in the dark suit, and Commodore Reische as the short man, center right, with his hands on his hips. (CMMSC.)

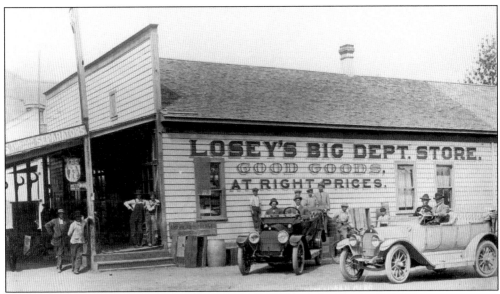

The painted sign on the wall, around 1914, says it all. On March 23, 1917, the prosperous store soon fell prey to a disastrous fire. The fire started in a nearby cigar store and burned all the adjoining businesses on that side of the street. The news reported that there was no fire apparatus. Citizens rallied to form a bucket brigade, but they could not diminish the wind-driven flames. (CMMSC.)

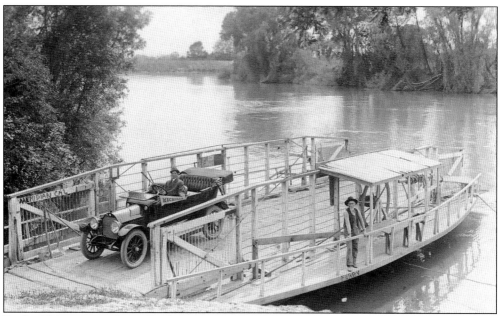

By the 20th century, the technology associated with a submerged cable to move the ferries across the river was more refined. The experience was a pleasant respite from the dusty roadways. In this 1915 photograph, the traveler is displaying a banner that says "Michigan." The days of the ferry were numbered, as bridges were forthcoming to accommodate vehicular and rail traffic. (CMMSC.)

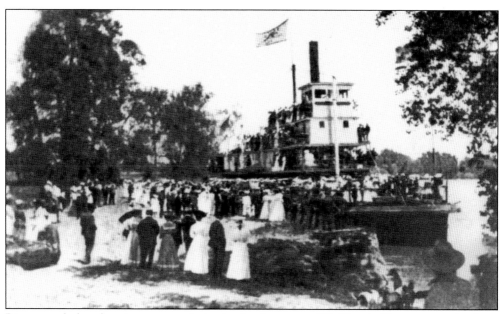

River travel played an important role in the development of California. Passage on a riverboat offered a level of comfort and refinement that was unmatched by a dusty, bumpy carriage or the confinement of railcars. This gathering at Meridian on May 19, 1911, conveys a convivial air borne of sophistication and opulence. The occasion was a huge picnic in Grimes. (CMMSC.)

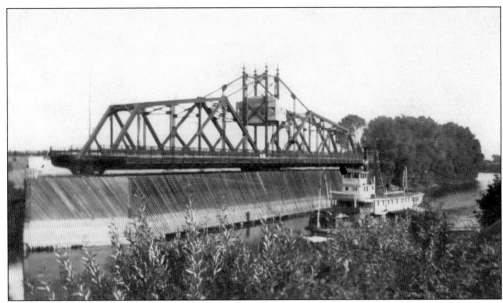

With the expansion of the Northern Electric Railroad spur between Marysville and Colusa, the rotating drawbridge, pictured in 1915, was constructed in 1913. It was designed to allow passage of commercial riverboats. The structure remained in place until the early 1970s, and two of the spires atop the control house are preserved in a local museum. (CMMSC.)

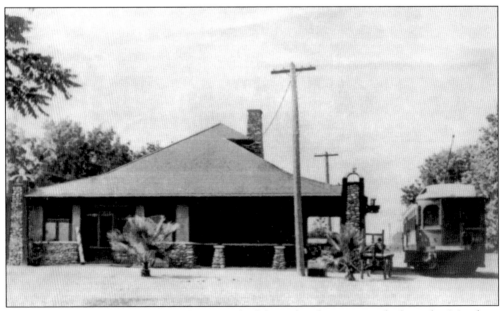

The distinctive craftsman styling and stonework of this railroad station was duplicated in Meridian, Live Oak, and Nicolaus by the Northern Electric Railway, which later became the Sacramento Northern Railway. Commuter rail service was available up until World War II. The station house in Meridian is used today as a private residence. (CMMSC.)

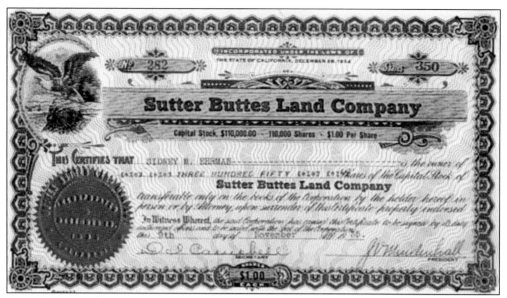

According to the face of this stock certificate, Sidney H. Erhman purchased 350 shares of the Sutter Buttes Land Company stock in November 1935. The firm was incorporated in 1934 by Meridian Farm Lands Company just south of nearby Meridian. While researching this book, this certificate was found listed for sale at a Web site that specializes in such historic documents. (Scripophily.com.)

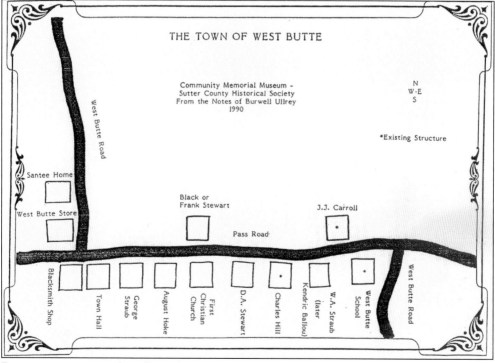

Distant memories work well in place of county documents. Although not to scale, this map details structures in the town of West Butte about a 100 years ago and will assist in orienting the old photographs of the town. It is over a half-mile between the intersections of West Butte and Pass Road. (CMMSC.)

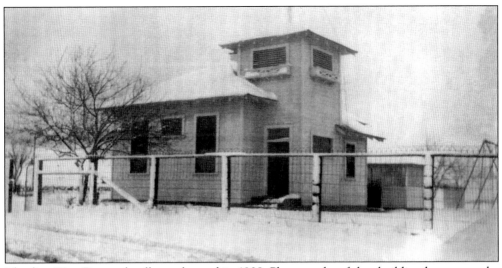

The first West Butte schoolhouse burned in 1908. Photographs of that building have yet to be found, but class photographs and school records have been archived. This one-room schoolhouse, pictured in the 1940s, was constructed in 1909 and used until 1943. After that, it was used as a rental home for 60 years and then donated to the Middle Mountain Foundation, which is working to restore it. (CMMSC.)

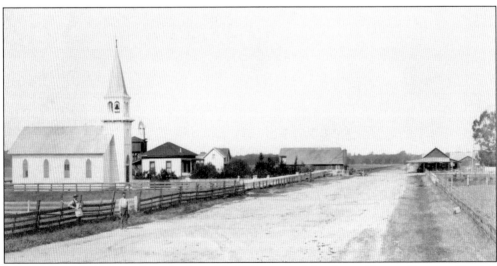

The words of "Old Squire" in the June 24, 1892, issue of the *Sutter County Farmer* offer this description: "We . . . arrive at West Butte. George Straub and sons run everything here, which consists of a general merchandise store, blacksmith, and repair shop. There are some neat residences, a public hall, and a fine church, but what its politicks were we did not find out." (Donna McMasters.)

This 1910 photograph is interesting because the old Slough schoolhouse still stands today, west across the Sutter bypass on private property along South Butte Road. According to statistics taken from Thompson and West, in 1879, Sutter County records tabulated 41 neighborhood schools serving 1,316 children. These schools were sometimes only 5 miles apart. Teachers' salaries averaged less than $500 a year. (CMMSC.)

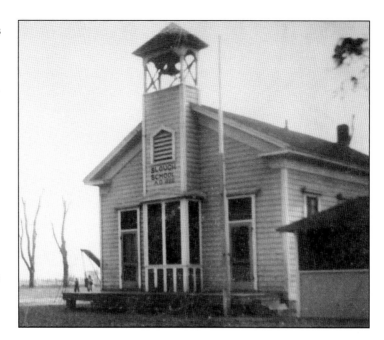

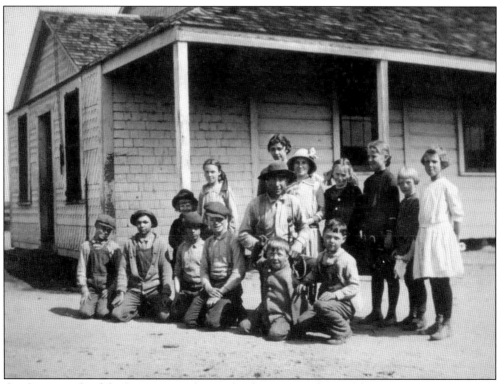

On the west side of the Buttes, Noyesberg School was across the road from the cemetery, midway between North Butte and Pass Roads. Records show it was used between 1875 and 1927. The last teacher there was Vera Carroll who grew up down the road in the West Butte area. The school was later used for years as a sheep barn. (CMMSC.)

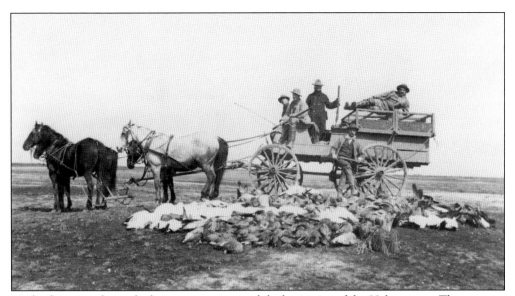

Market hunting of waterfowl was common around the beginning of the 20th century. The cages on the back of the wagon were for live decoys whose wings were clipped. In this 1916 photograph, the day's catch was spread out for an unidentified photographer in southern Butte County. The limit was 50 birds per hunter, and they could make a dollar for each bird. The practice was outlawed in 1923. (*A Jewel in the Pacific Flyway* by John Cowan.)

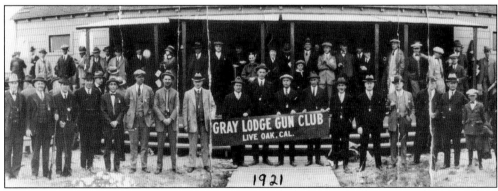

The Gray Lodge Gun Club was organized in 1921, and a lodge was built on grounds just north of the Buttes. The structure burned down in 1929 and was never rebuilt. They decided to sell the land to the state in 1931 to be used for the first waterfowl refuge in the Sacramento Valley. (*A Jewel in the Pacific Flyway* by John Cowan.)

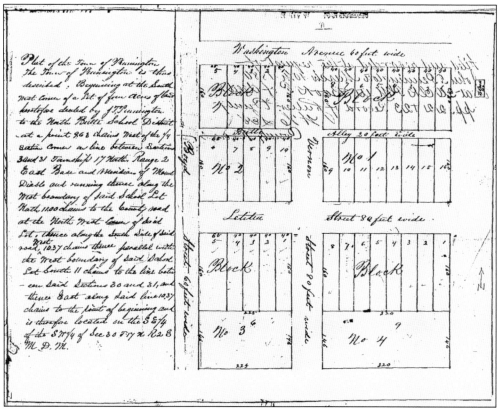

A copy of the original plat map of Pennington reveals 39 lots, laid out 160 feet deep, and most with 40-foot frontages. Street names proposed were Washington, Letitia, and Boyd. On the back of the page, the writing, which shows through, says, "Filed and recorded at the request of John T. Pennington, March 10th 1880." (Sutter County public records.)

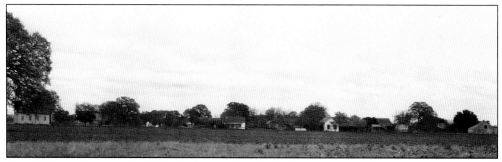

North Butte photographer Billy McMurtry lived a half-mile west of Pennington. In this 1915 photograph, the People's Church, pictured at the left, is the most prominent feature from this distance. Old Squire's newspaper account states, "On arriving at Pennington we find Bud Kingsbury doing a good mercantile business, the two blacksmith shops lively with work." (Brian McMurtry.)

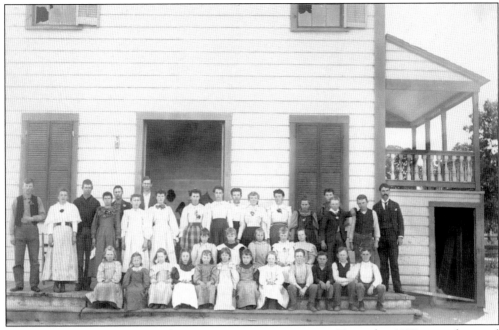

Pennington School was unique due to its two-story construction. Erected in 1877, it was financed in part by the local Odd Fellows Lodge who used the second floor as a meeting hall. It remained in use until 1954, and many area residents have memories about attending the school. The broken windows in this undated photograph are intriguing. (Brian McMurtry.)

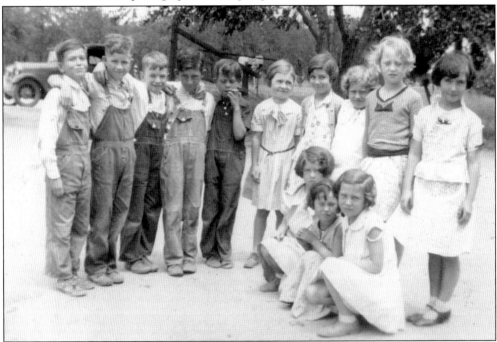

This must be after school—everyone is so relaxed. "My Sis, Alice, is kneeling in the middle. That's Jim Spilman in the dark bibs. Betty Brady is the tall one, and that's Wilma Adams on the right," reported Barbara, who donated this picture. (Barbara Dow Kamilos.)

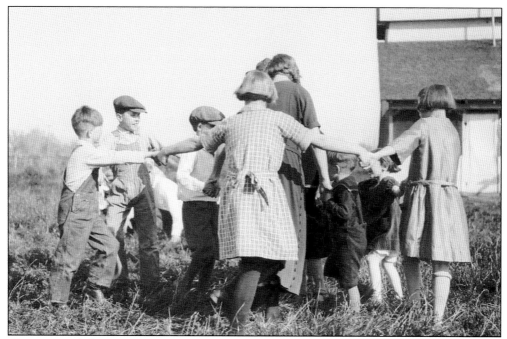

"Ring around the Rosie" is a fun way to get all ages acquainted and playing together. Little information was available with this photograph but the preschoolers in the group suggest that this is a family gathering. The dark grass underfoot looks green but the trees in the distance are bare, which means that this was a late winter or early spring day. (Brian McMurtry.)

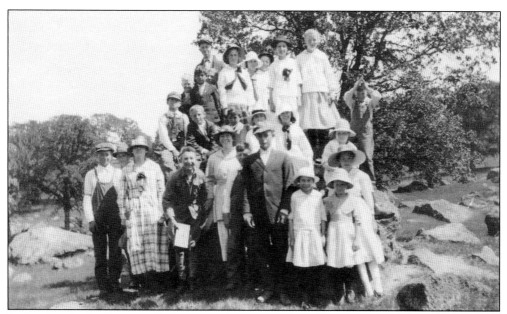

Springtime in the Buttes is the best time for a picnic. It is all so green and not that hot. While everyone gathered for the photograph, the kids have fun by climbing up on one of the rocks. The photograph was taken around 1910 at Lena Hubbs' school picnic. (Barbara Dow Kamilos.)

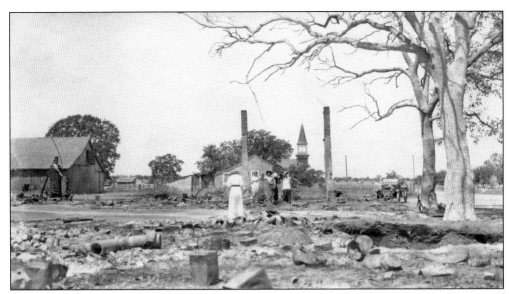

Some tourists stopped to take a photograph amidst the charred ruins at Pennington after most of the town burned down. The church was set back far enough and was untouched by the flames, as was the schoolhouse, which was behind the photographer. Both of those structures remained until the 1950s. Museum records date this tragedy to 1907. (Mary Spilman Crane.)

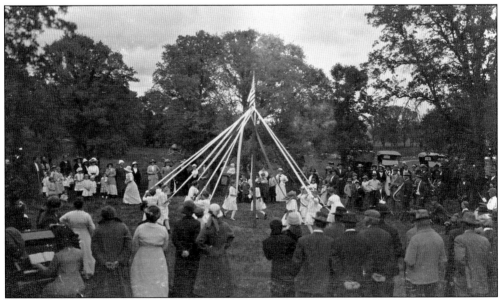

This maypole dance event drew quite a crowd. If it was held in May, as is traditional, this was a particularly long and cool spring season. The grass is still dark and green and everyone is bundled up in their coats and hats under gray, cloudy skies. Note the organ player and the brass band. (Brian McMurtry.)

EIGHTH ANNUAL
Sutter County Farm Bureau
PICNIC
DOW GROVE
Saturday, May 12, 1928

PROGRAM

10:00 A. M.—Limited High School Track Meet.

10:45 A. M.—Children's Races.

12:00 M.—Lunch.

1:00 P. M.—Horseshoe Tournament.

1:30 P. M.—Unlimited High School Track Meet.

1:30 to 3:00 P. M.—Farm Home Department Exhibits. Live Stock Exhibits.

2:15 to 6:15 P. M.—Free Dancing.
Music by Wagner's Orchestra.

8:30 P. M.—Big Evening Dance.
Music by Wagner's Orchestra.

(over)

(BRING THIS PROGRAM WITH YOU.)

Sutter County Farm Bureau Picnic
TRACK MEET
May 12, 1928

OFFICIALS

Director of the Meet—H. A. Hunter.
Referee—Loyd Hewitt.
Starter—C. H. Straub.
Clerk of Course—H. A. Hunter.
Timers—E. R. Hansen, F. R. Havens, H. A. Speer.
Marshals—A. Lamme, Buck Manford.
Announcer—H. B. Jeffrey.
Scorer—H. A. Wells.
Press Steward—Otis Sweetland.

Inspectors—E. R. Brubaker, S. Stephens, John Wolstenholm.
Judge of Finish—E. S. Wadsworth, Chief; Arthur Coats, H. Ramsdell, E. H. Cobeen, Moore Metteer.
Field Judges—F. C. Darby, Chief; E. Hauck, H. Cobeen, H. Eachus, Floyd Wolstenholm, John Clayton.
Track Committee—P. B. Vantress, T. L. Nelson, Leo Wadsworth, H. A. Hunter.

TRACK EVENTS

LIMITED MEET

100 YARD DASH
F. Rollins, L. O.; Pierce, L. O.; Danielson, L. O.; Gray, Y. C.; Ulrey, Y. C.; Sandow, Y. C.; Spears, S.; Reische, S.

120 YARD HURDLES
Cooper, L. O.; Bruce, Y. C.; Barron, Y. C.; Wallace, S.; Reische, S.

220 YARD DASH
Pierce, L. O.; Heilman, L. O.; Jenkins, L. O.; Gray, Y. C.; Ulrey, Y. C.; Sandow, Y. C.; E. Nall, S.

UNLIMITED MEET

100 YARD DASH
Fairlee, L. O.; Blazer, Y. C.; Otis, Y. C.; Phillips, S.; Summy, S.

120 YARD HURDLES
Cobeen, L. O.; Fairlee, L. O.; Hanawalt, Y. C.; Kozlosky, Y. C.; Catlett, S.; Frye, S.

880 YARD RUN
Hinshaw, L. O.; Walton, L. O.; Rollins, L. O.; Baker, Y. C.; Carnegie, Y. C.; Sherman, Y. C.; V. Nall, S.; Staas, S.

220 YARD DASH
Blazer, Y. C.; Otis, Y. C.; Phillips, S.; Summy, S.; Paxton, S.

440 YARD RUN
Hinshaw, L. O.; Walton, L. O.; Rollins, L. O.; Webdell, Y. C.; Queen, Y. C.; Foley, Y. C.; Rawley, S.; V. Nall, S.; Staas, S.

220 YARD HURDLES
Cobeen, L. O.; Vantress, L. O.; Webdell, Y. C.; Sherman, Y. C.; Catlett, S.; Messick, S.

1 MILE RUN
Metteer, L. O.; Vantress, L. O.; Zirklee, L. O.; Carnegie, Y. C.; Foley, Y. C.; Baker, Y. C.; La Montagne, S.

FIELD EVENTS

HIGH JUMP
Ott, L. O.; F. Rollins, L. O.; Jenkins, L. O.; Bruce, Y. C.; Ulrey, Y. C.; Sandow, Y. C.; Spears, S.; Nall, S.

SHOT PUT
Danielson, L. O.; Pierce, L. O.; Westlund, Y. C.; Barron, Y. C.; Wallace, S.; Nall, S.

BROAD JUMP
Heilman, L. O.; Ott, L. O.; Jenkins, L. O.; Davis, Y. C.; Bruce, Y. C.; Barron, Y. C.; Spears, S.

DISCUS THROW
F. Rollins, L. O.; Heilman, L. O.; Danielson, L. O.; Davis, Y. C.; Gray, Y. C.; Westlund, Y. C.; Wallace, S.; Reische, S.

POLE VAULT
Cobeen, L. O.; Vantress, L. O.; Tomasovich, L. O.; Hanawalt, Y. C.; Ohleyer, S.; Paxton, S.; Nall, S.

HIGH JUMP
Cobeen, L. O.; Fairlee, L. O.; Webdell, Y. C.; Queen, Y. C.; Nelson, V. C.; Catlett, S.; Frye, S.; Paxton, S.

SHOT PUT
Cobeen, L. O.; Roulsten, L. O.; Smith, L. O.; Kozlosky, Y. C.; Foley, Y. C.; Baker, Y. C.; Rawley, S.; Messick, S.; Mayfield, S.

BROAD JUMP
Metteer, L. O.; Roulsten, L. O.; Otis, Y. C.; Blazer, Y. C.; Phillips, S.; Summy, S.; Messick, S.

JAVELIN THROW
Tomasovich, L. O.; Walton, L. O.; Kozlosky, Y. C.; Ohleyer, S.; Frye, S.; La Montagne, S.

DISCUS THROW
Smith, L. O.; Rollins, L. O.; Hinshaw, L. O.; Nelson, Y. C.; Hanawalt, Y. C.; Rawley, S.; Mayfield, S.; La Montagne, S.

INDEPENDENT, YUBA CITY, CAL.

Each May, the Dow Grove Farm Bureau picnics were big events. Locals remember the event recurring up until World War II. The programs shown here document a full day of competitive track and field events, exhibits, and dancing into the evening. This aerial photograph of the meadow, alongside Pennington Road, reveals the impression of the quarter mile oval racetrack in the lower portion of the clearing. Flourishing pasture grasses have long since obscured any evidence of it after this photograph was taken. (CMMSC.)

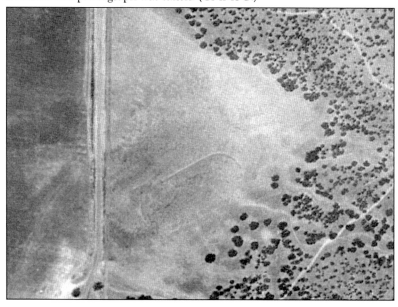

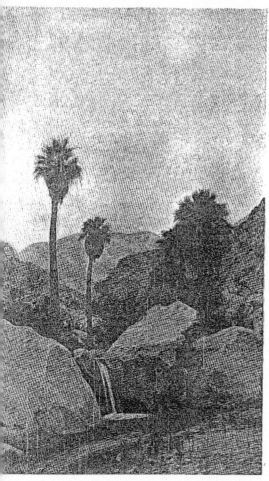

A Palm Canyon in Southern California
(See pages 51 and 69)

ABBOTT

64895

REPORT

OF

STATE PARK SURVEY

OF

CALIFORNIA

Prepared for the
CALIFORNIA STATE PARK COMMISSION
BY
FREDERICK LAW OLMSTED

CALIFORNIA STATE PRINTING OFFICE
SACRAMENTO, 1929

This State Parks Survey of California was completed in response to a $6,000,000 State Park Bond overwhelmingly passed by the voters in 1927. The report, directed by Frederick Law Olmsted in 1928, cataloged sites around California that were "suitable and desirable . . . (for) . . . conserving and utilizing the scenic and recreational resources of the state." Urgent concerns emphasized were: to protect "natural assets" and "to curb and limit the activities of exploiters who would destroy the birthright of their successor." A list of 125 projects for consideration included a photograph and listing for a "Pioneer Memorial Park" in the Marysville Butte region, for historic and scenic value and for picnics. (California State Parks, Northern Buttes District.)

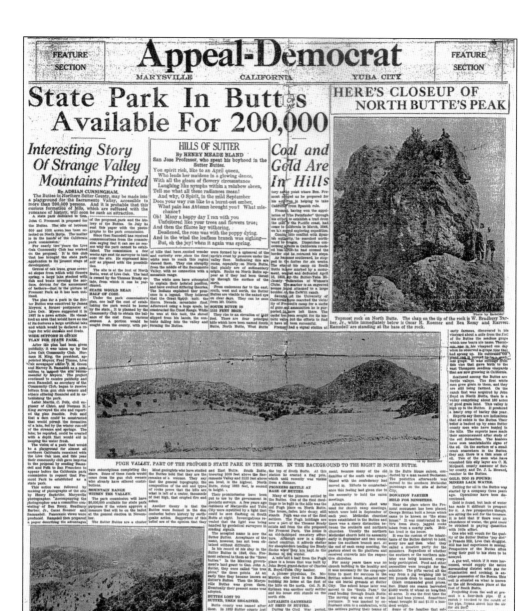

This newspaper article from 1928 championed a proposed state park "dedicated to John C. Fremont" in the Buttes that would include a dam to create a "large artificial lake . . . fed by winter run-off of streams and springs . . . and provide a recreation playground for all of northern California!" The article reported that the plan was conceived by James Meyers, a former postmaster in Live Oak, promoted by the Live Oak Community Club, and had wide support. (MMF, donated by Robert Ramsdell.)

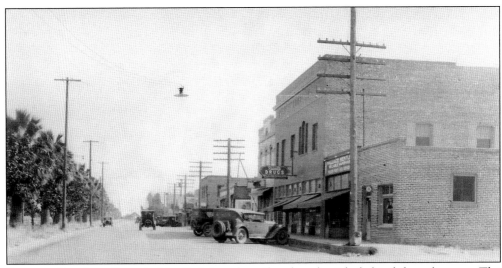

Stores on Broadway Street in Live Oak face the railroad tracks right behind the palm trees. The business district did not grow much beyond what is pictured here in 1925, because the speed and convenience of the train and the automobile meant that it was no longer a day's ride to Marysville or Yuba City. (CMMSC.)

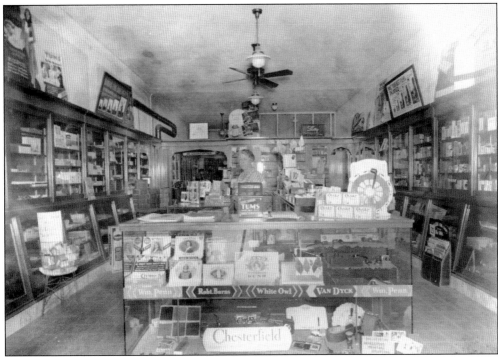

In the robust and booming times that preceded the Depression, this Live Oak pharmacy was packed with merchandise. Many of the labels look familiar to people today. A note on the picture's reverse names the merchant as Pearl Higgins. Her husband had a doctor's office in the back room. One informant identified the clerk as Mrs. Hill. (CMMSC.)

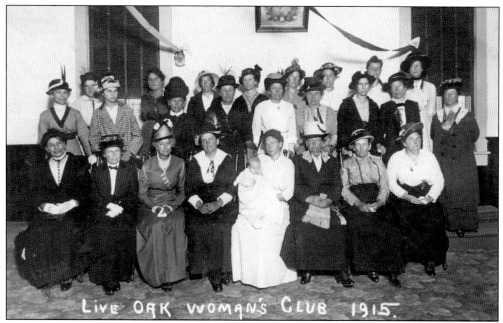

The Live Oak Woman's Club has a long history in this community. Several of the older women remember their mothers' involvement in the organization with pride. In the photograph, taken around 1915, Mary Spilman Crane pointed out her grandmother, second from the left in the front, as being the president the year this photograph was taken. (CMMSC.)

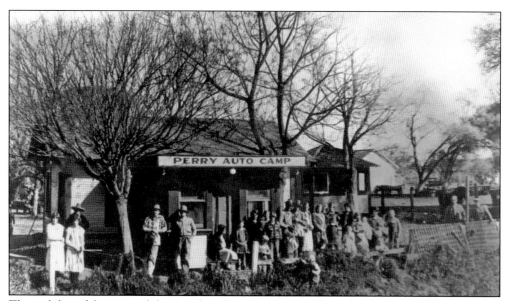

The mobility of the automobile contributed to a more accessible mode of accommodating travelers than hotels in town. Auto camps sprang up for those with tents, and many offered small cabins, like the Perry Auto Camp, just south of Live Oak, pictured around 1935. The Depression in the 1930s brought many travelers who were displaced or who followed the agricultural harvests for work. (CMMSC.)

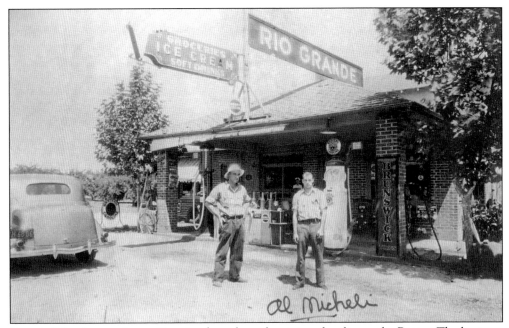

Pasquini's has been at Lomo Crossing for so long that it is as familiar as the Buttes. The business thrived for years as a market and gas stop between Live Oak and Yuba City. It has been a restaurant for about 30 years now and is still operated by the Pasquini and Micheli families. The drive-thru portion of the structure was enclosed to provide additional seating and the exposed brick retains its historic appeal. (Pasquini's.)

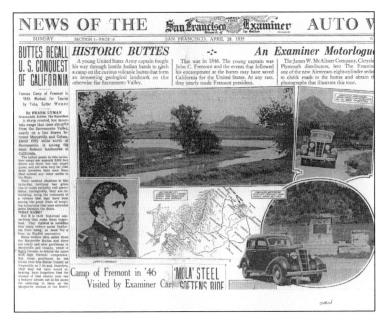

A tour around the Buttes has always been a pleasant springtime diversion. Over the years many articles have been found similar to the one pictured, inviting the public to enjoy the historic and scenic features of the unique Buttes landscape. In this 1935 article, a San Francisco Chrysler-Plymouth dealer loaned the Examiner a new car to test drive provided it was included in the travelogue. (CMMSC.)

Seven

FARMS AND RANCHES

The California Gold Rush, during the last half of the 19th century, financed the Civil War and fueled an industrial revolution that expanded the American economy. It was a time when industry and enterprise were paramount. Long hours and hard work were a way of life, and to own land offered one a chance to make something worthwhile of his life. The broad Sacramento Valley, with its oak woodlands and flat grasslands and nearby waterways, offered mild winters and long summers that provided eight months of growing season.

Settlers took to clearing the land along the rivers and cutting timber for steam-driven riverboats that plied the navigable waterways. Cattle and horses were grazed on the expansive grass savannas. Much of these wild grasslands were scythed and sold to feed the packhorses and mules that pulled the freight wagons and stagecoaches.

Lithographs from Thompson and West's 1879 *History of Sutter County* included herein, admittedly furnish idealized depictions of early farm life, but great effort was applied in this artwork to capture the essence of the early horse-drawn threshers and harvesters circling outward amid vast fields of hay.

Vineyards and fruit trees were planted around the Spanish missions that were constructed from San Diego in 1769 up to Solano in 1823. John Sutter planted many varieties to promote the agricultural opportunity to newcomers. Grains, grapes, fruits, nuts, and vegetables have all flourished around the Buttes.

It may have been the Gold Rush that initially brought most of these families to California; still today one wonders if the proximity of the Sutter Buttes may have prompted many of them to select this remote setting to build a life. Such sentiment is not documented, but the old photographs and prints wordlessly convey this feeling. Note the presence of the Buttes behind most of the farms depicted in Thompson and West. Conversations with family descendents open up feelings in all generations of a connection to the landscape from nostalgic recollections to photograph collections to art on display. Why would our forefathers feel differently about the Buttes than people do today?

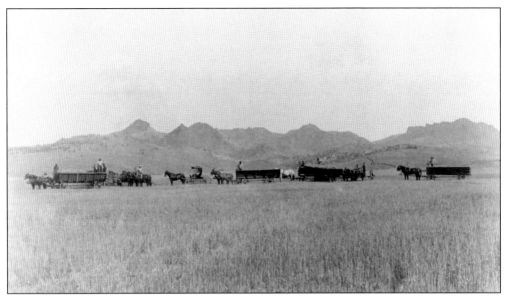

Complex horse- or mule-drawn harvesting equipment enabled landowners around 1900 to harvest vast quantities of hay and grain. Mild, wet winters and long, rain-free California summers limited early entrepreneurs to grazing livestock or growing grasses and grains. The Brady Ranch pictured here around 1920 is on the west side of the Buttes. (CMMSC.)

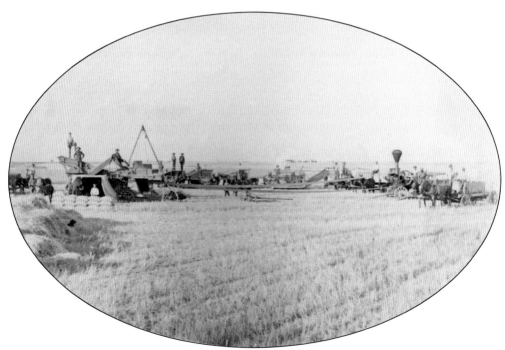

Compare this photograph taken around 1900 to the background detail of the lithograph depicting the Graves Ranch on page 62. The grain was bagged and the hay was stacked. It was hot dusty work for a lot of men and equipment. (CMMSC.)

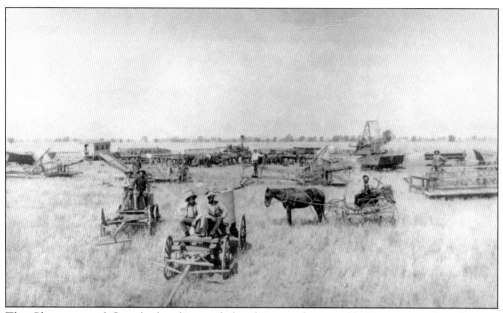

The Channon and Ormsby heading and threshing outfit assembled its crew and equipment near Live Oak for a photograph in early July 1906. There appear to be a dozen workers posing for the photograph. The windowed trailer at the left rear is a chuck wagon, where everyone is fed. (CMMSC.)

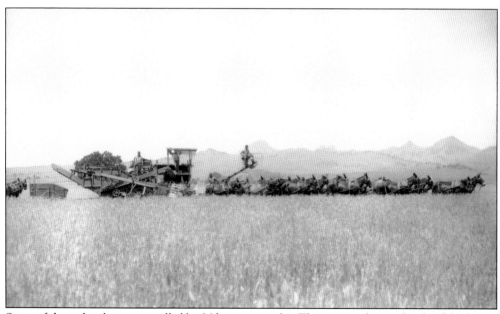

Some of these threshers were pulled by 26 horses or mules. This was on the north side of the Buttes around 1900. A pause in the work offered respite for a drink of water and a brief rest. (CMMSC.)

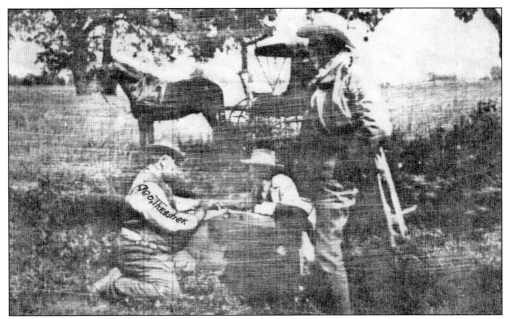

Engineering and financing a canal system to irrigate the dry grassland savannas of the Sacramento Valley was a monumental step towards developing productive farmlands around the Buttes. Pictured here around 1904 are the principals in the early contract signing: George Thresher, Duncan McCallum to his right, and standing was Judge E. A. Bridgeford, president of the Butte County Canal Company. By 1911, the firm consolidated with another enterprise to become the Sutter Butte Canal Company. Their water channels from the Feather River can be found on some of the old 7.5-minute USGS topographical maps. The open pastureland was then suitable for growing orchards and rice. (Both, CMMSC.)

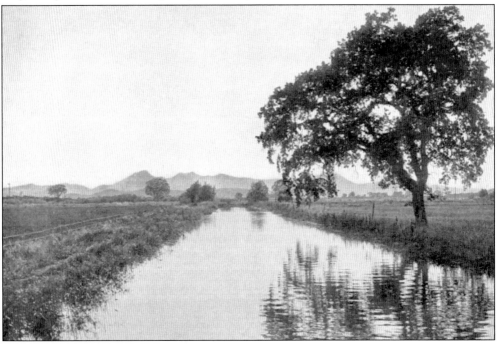

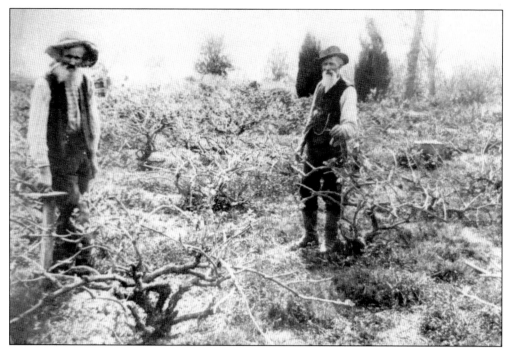

William Thompson (left) and his son, George, standing here around 1880 amid their grapevines, southeast of the Buttes, propagated the world-famous Thompson seedless grape. The industry started from three cuttings. Grapes without seeds revolutionized the raisin grape industry. Within a few years, farmers throughout the valley were growing these Thompson seedless grapes. (CMMSC.)

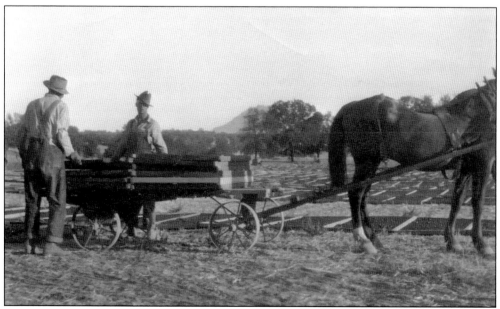

Thompson seedless grapes were spread out on trays in the sun to dry into raisins. Around 1920, on the north side of the Buttes, Harold Hubbs is facing the camera. (Barbara Dow Kamilos.)

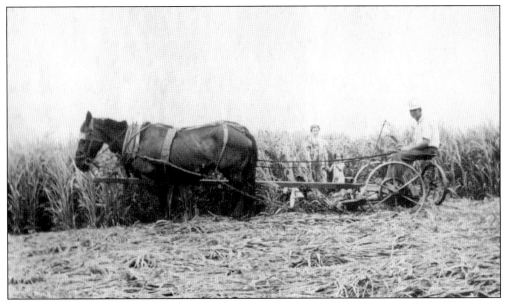

Around 1925, Irving Dow operates a mower to cut Sudan grass. "It was never baled," Barbara remembers. "We fed it to the sheep." Irving was Barbara's father. (Barbara Dow Kamilos.)

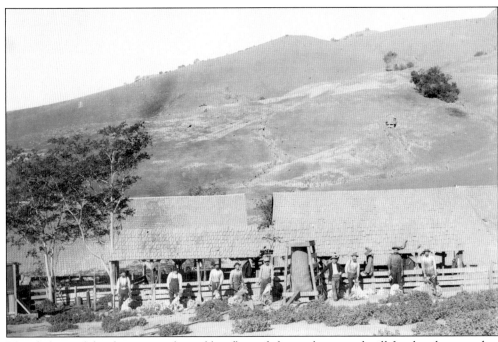

The clicking of the shears was silenced briefly, and the workers stood still for the photographer around 1900 at the Brockman Ranch off Pass Road. The clipped wool goes into the tall gunnysack in the wooden framework. (CMMSC.)

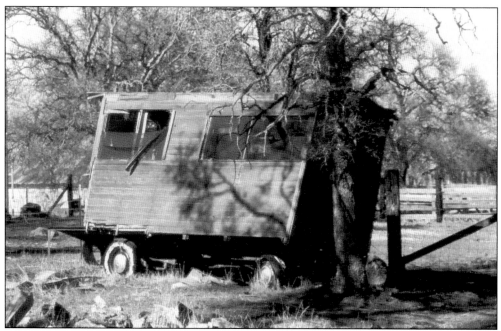

These old sheepherder camp wagons used to be scattered around the Buttes so the shepherds could sleep near the sheep. Barking sheep dogs would alert them of predators. The wagons had a small wood stove, a table, and a cushioned bench for sitting and sleeping. This derelict, pictured in 1978, was built on an old truck chassis and had everything but headroom. (Mike Hubbartt.)

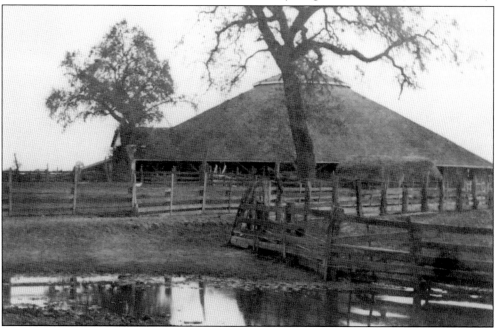

Verna McLean Sexton wrote that tourists used to be directed out to see their unusual round barn at the foot of North Butte (pictured here in 1900). Built in 1891, according to the local museum, it was 180 feet in diameter with a hayloft overhead that was 96 feet across. The structure could hold 4,000 sheep. (CMMSC.)

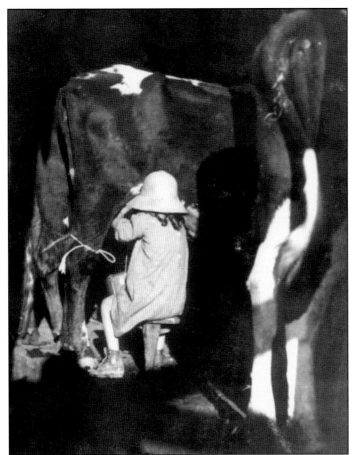

To four-year-old Edwina Dean, milking was just another chore as part of life on the farm. But to her proud parents, it was a priceless moment captured on film. As this book went to press, Edwina had just celebrated her 100th birthday. (Margit Sands.)

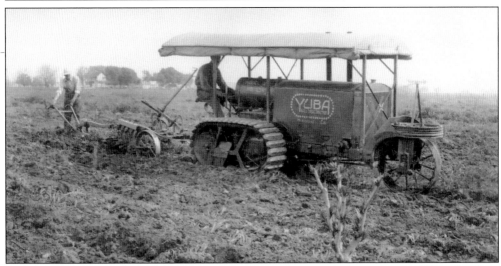

Between 1910 and 1920, tractors began to replace the horse-pulled equipment. The technology of steam engines was replaced by gas and diesel, which reduced weight and increased pulling power. The Yuba Ball tractor pictured here in 1920, used by the Weichert and Heier families, was manufactured locally in Marysville. (John Heier.)

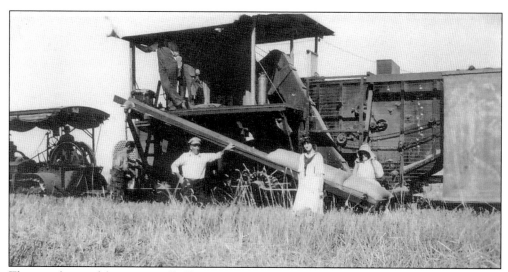

The complexity of the tractor-pulled harvesting equipment is revealed in this photograph. There are three sacks of grain that slid down the chute behind the pretty lady, around 1920. (John Heier.)

Where Pennington Road turns north is the site of the old Vantress Poultry Ranch. The long, white shelters in this aerial photograph housed 45,000 chickens. At one time, a staff of 18 people developed breeding stock for egg-laying and meat chickens that were shipped throughout the western United States. The tree-covered hill at the bottom of the 1958 photograph has since been excavated as part of a quarry operation. (Rick Powell.)

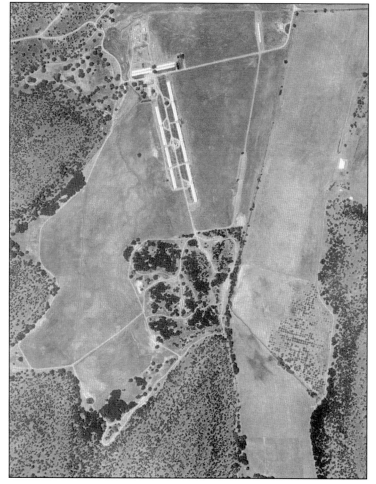

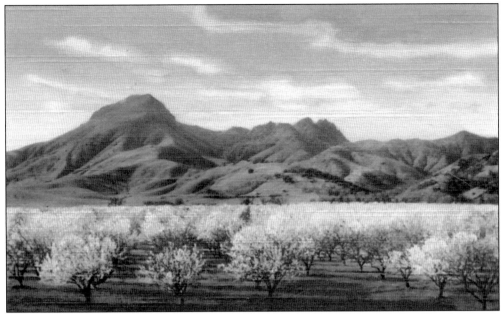

An old, penny postcard from 1940 captures the contrast of blossoming orchards in front with the treeless contours of the Buttes' southern slopes. Fruit and nut orchards have flourished in the last century. The allure of blossom time always entices travelers to tour the roads around the mountain. (Dorothy Jenkins Ross.)

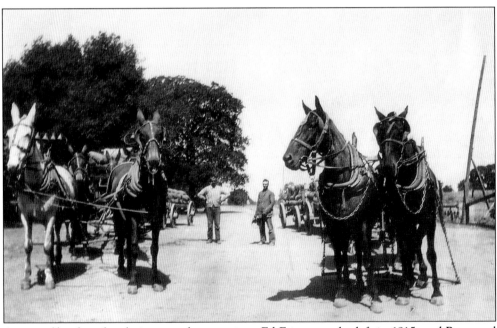

A year of hard work culminates at harvest time. Ed Frieze, on the left in 1915, and Raymond Redhair, on the right, along with two teams of horses, are preparing to haul harvested almonds to the train station in Live Oak. Some families invested in hullers to crack open the nuts. A load of meats is worth more than nuts in the shell. (Dorothy Rae Redhair Coats.)

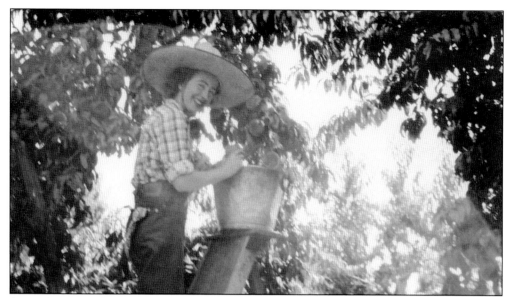

Sutter County orchards have a national reputation. Our central valley grows the food on America's tables. Picking peaches from atop a ladder in 1935, young Dorothy Jenkins looks like a model in an advertisement. She is now in her mid-90s. (Dorothy Jenkins Ross.)

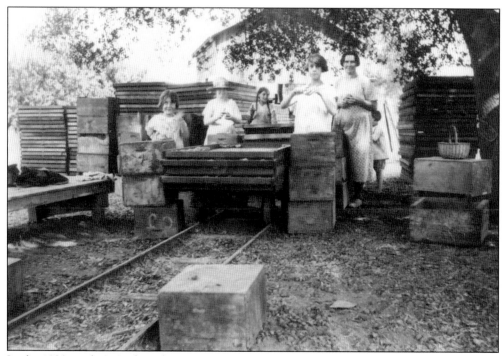

In the 1930s and 1940s, fruit drying was still a family operation. The Jenkins family's work area was under the shade of a huge blue oak where they sliced and laid out peaches on the trays and pushed the little rail cart out to the drying area in the sun. Some of this old equipment is displayed in the local museum. (Dorothy Jenkins Ross.)

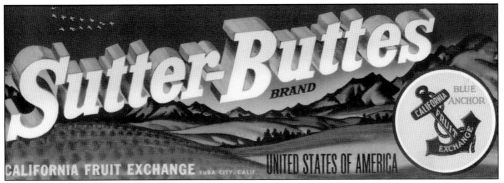

Even 100 years ago, marketing executives understood the importance of a recognizable symbol to retain consumer support. The California Fruit Exchange, based in Sacramento, used the blue anchor label for years. They knew the Buttes would engender immediate recognition of their products. (CMMSC.)

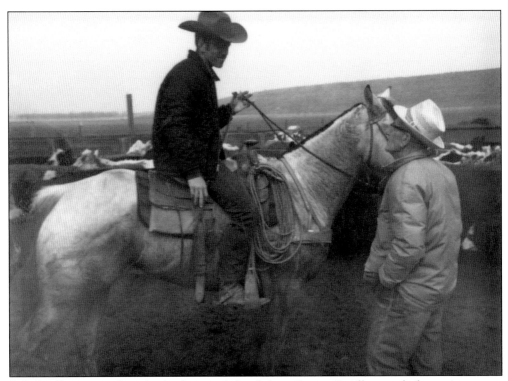

Bob Steidlmayer, on horseback, chats with his father, George Steidlmayer, before going out to move cattle on the west side of the Buttes in 1965. Bob's son, Marty, now lives in the picturesque family home tucked back against the hillside. The Steidlmayers have a long farming and ranching history in the Colusa area. Marty occasionally leads public hikes and has many stories about growing up in the Buttes. (Marty Steidlmayer.)

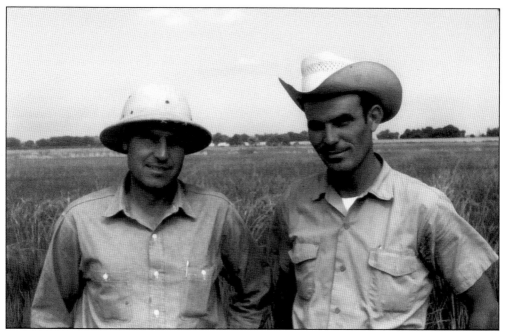

The Tarke brothers, Louis and Richard, are pictured here in the late 1960s. They have farmed a variety of produce over the years but are probably best known for bean production. After harvest time, small gunnysacks of Tarke beans are for sale at the family warehouse. (David Tarke.)

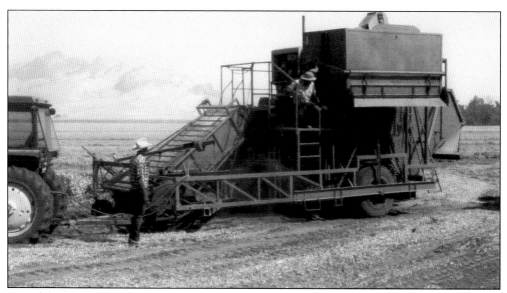

A work break in 1965 offers readers an opportunity to casually inspect the Tarke brothers' Harris bean harvester. It was custom-made locally to their specifications. Richard Tarke's son, David, remembers that when his dad, pictured in the cowboy hat, drove the tractor too fast, his uncle Louis, pictured on the back in the campaign helmet, would throw a dirt clod against the tractor to slow him down. (David Tarke.)

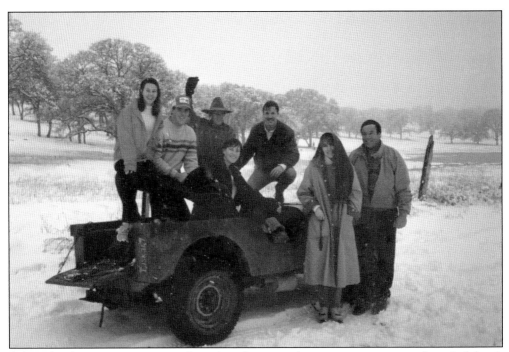

A long, hard season or even a tough workweek is enough reason to get away and unwind, but it is great to do it in the "back 40," especially in a snowfall. Buttes' families appreciate their places and get together to share special moments with friends and family. John and Kathy Heier were pictured in 2001 in the old ranch jeep. (John Heier.)

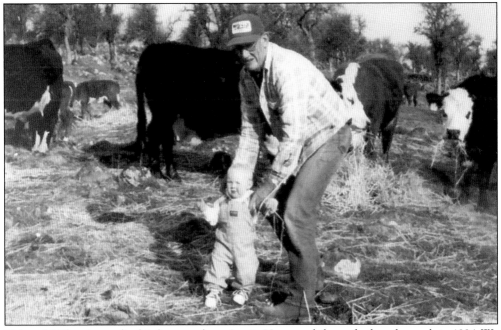

Calvert McPherrin steadies his first grandson, Austin Harvey, while out feeding the cattle in 1994. We first saw Calvert as a youngster in his bibs at the same ranch about 75 years ago on page 69. Farming and ranching—it can be washed off your boots but it stays in your blood. (Calvert McPherrin.)

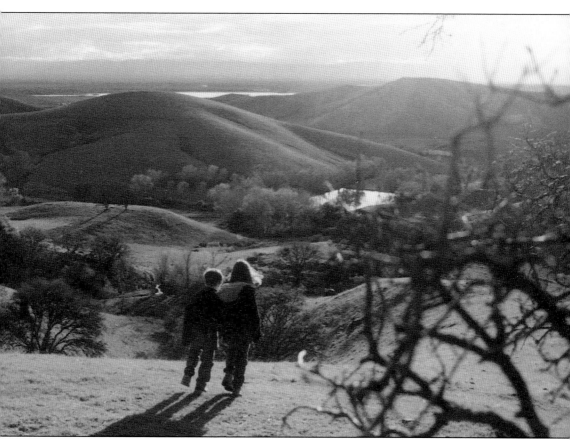

The future looks bright for Riley and Casey Steidlmayer pictured here in 2000. The reality is that the Sutter Buttes may look like a park, but it has always taken a lot of hard work and other farming or financial enterprises to maintain these ranches. Carrying on this ranch work is a family legacy that comes from the heart. Some youngsters leave before they gain this perspective. (Marty Steidlmayer.)

DISCOVER THOUSANDS OF LOCAL HISTORY BOOKS FEATURING MILLIONS OF VINTAGE IMAGES

Arcadia Publishing, the leading local history publisher in the United States, is committed to making history accessible and meaningful through publishing books that celebrate and preserve the heritage of America's people and places.

Find more books like this at
www.arcadiapublishing.com

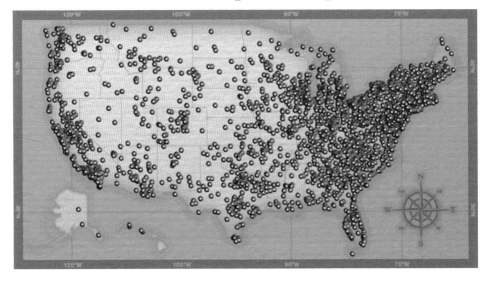

Search for your hometown history, your old stomping grounds, and even your favorite sports team.

Consistent with our mission to preserve history on a local level, this book was printed in South Carolina on American-made paper and manufactured entirely in the United States. Products carrying the accredited Forest Stewardship Council (FSC) label are printed on 100 percent FSC-certified paper.

MADE IN THE
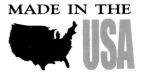